Pronunciation of English for
Brazilian
learners

PronPack 6
Pronunciation of English for Brazilian learners

- Resource book for teachers of English
- Activities for Brazilian learners
- Easy-to-follow presentation notes
- Print and screen-friendly worksheets
- Extra resources online at PronPack.com

Mark Hancock

Hancock McDonald
ENGLISH LANGUAGE TEACHING

PronPack 6
Pronunciation of English for Brazilian learners

Mark Hancock

Published by **Hancock McDonald ELT**
Chester. CH1 2AW UK
www.hancockmcdonald.com

First Published 2021
ISBN: 9781838404000

Author: Mark Hancock
Editor: Annie McDonald
Consultant: Ricardo Sili
Design: Amanda Hancock
Graphics: Heliographic
Illustration: Mark Hancock
Images: Shutterstock.com
Audio: Mark Hancock and Annie McDonald

Contents

PronPack 6 Pronunciation of English for Brazilian Learners

PronPack 6 Activities and Worksheets

The PronPack Sound Charts

About the Author

Map of the book

LESSON		TEACHING FOCUS	ACTIVITY
6.1	Kim and Tim	Nasal consonants /m/, /n/, and /ŋ/ at the end of words	Rap and Map
6.2	Rabbit in a Hat	The phoneme /r/ at the beginning of words	Minimal pairs and rap
6.3	Better Call Paul	The phoneme /l/ at the end of words	Minimal pairs and rap
6.4	Teas or Cheese?	When /t/ and /d/ become /tʃ/ and /dʒ/ before /i/	Minimal pairs and map
6.5	Thin and Then	The phonemes /θ/ and /ð/, and alternatives	Rap and board game
6.6	Bear or Pear?	The phonemes /p/, /t/ and /k/	Rap and minimal pair game
6.7	Piece or Peas?	The phonemes /s/ and /z/ at the end of words	Minimal pairs and map
6.8	Smart Bart	Initial consonant clusters with /s/	Listening maze and minimal pairs
6.9	Cough or Coffee?	Adding a vowel or reducing a vowel at the end of words	Minimal pairs and question and answers
6.10	Live or Leave?	Distinguishing /ɪ/ and /iː/	Rap and minimal pairs
6.11	Brad or Bread?	Distinguishing /æ/ and /e/	Rap and minimal pair game
6.12	River of Vowels	The spelling and pronunciation of the alphabet vowels	Joke and Maze
6.13	Money to Burn	Pronouncing the vowel phoneme /ɜː/	Rap and maze
6.14	Ambitions	Consonant spellings of /tʃ/, /ʃ/ and /ʒ/	Rap and maze
6.15	Wanted, Needed	Pronouncing the past tense suffix –ed	Rap and maze
6.16	Stress Wall	Word stress in cognates; syllable reduction	Joke and maze
6.17	Tennis Shoes	Word stress in compound nouns	Choral chant/drill
6.18	I love you	Tonic stress	Choral chant/drill
PronPack Sound Charts		A teaching and reference tool for the individual vowel sounds of English Phonemic charts with key words for the symbols used in this book, as well as those often used in American publications for comparison.	

Introduction

What is PronPack?

PronPack is a growing collection of innovative teachers' resource materials for working on English pronunciation in the classroom. **PronPacks 1-4** won the 2018 *ELTons Award for Innovation in Teacher Resources*, as well as the *English Speaking Union's 2018 English Language Award runner-up for teacher resources.*

What is Pronunciation of English for Brazilian learners?

PronPack 6: Pronunciation of English for Brazilian Learners

contains English pronunciation materials for teachers working with Portuguese-speaking learners from Brazil. The lessons focus on aspects of pronunciation which such learners often find difficult because they are very different in English and Portuguese. Many of these are at the level of consonant and vowel sounds, but there are also some are above the individual sound level.

What is the philosophy behind the PronPack approach?

In my view, the most important reason to teach pronunciation is to help your students understand and be understood. For this reason, the lessons in this book focus on pronunciation issues which are most likely to affect intelligibility. The objective is not for your students to sound like native speakers of any specific variety of English, but to be better communicators in a world where English is a global Lingua Franca.

What materials are in the book?

The book contains copiable worksheets for the students and teacher's notes for you. The teacher's notes highlight the teaching focus, minimum level, and indicate printing requirements and audio files for each activity.

The notes include some background to the pronunciation point plus a language comparison between Brazilian Portuguese and English. This is followed with step by step instructions for using the lesson in class.

The student worksheets in **PronPack 6** are available to download from the support website and can be printed out, or alternatively you can project them. If you are teaching online, you can send the worksheet to your students electronically or show them via screenshare.

What will I find on the support website www.pronpack.com?
The website *www.pronpack.com* provides additional resources for users of *PronPack 6*, including:

- Electronic versions of the *worksheets* for printing or projecting

- Downloadable *MP3 audio files* for those who wish to use them

- Access to general support materials for the PronPack collection, including the *PronPack Sound Charts* and other *extras*.

What are the audio files for?
There are audio files for most of the lessons. Teachers can use these if they are not confident about their own pronunciation. However, you can model the materials yourself instead of using the audio files, and this is usually the better option. For the raps in this book, there are two *Audio* versions, *1* (voice and music), or *2* just the backing music for you to speak over. If you do this, it is wise to practice a couple of times before class so that you know where the difficulties lie. Remember these are raps, not songs. You can use your normal speaking voice, you don't have to sing!

What level are the activities designed for?
The minimum level is indicated in the teacher's notes for each workout, but for almost all of the lessons, it is pre-intermediate, or A2. But remember that this is a minimum level. An activity which is suitable for a pre-intermediate learner is often just as valuable for an upper intermediate learner – pronunciation often lags behind other competences.

Are the activities aimed at a specific age group and class size?
The activities are not aimed at a specific age group and should benefit young learners and adults alike. The activities in this book should function in any size of class, but there are a lot of raps which are usually less fun for very small classes or one to one.

Do students have to know the phonemic alphabet?

No. Although phonemic symbols sometimes appear on the worksheets, being able to understand them is never essential for the successful completion of the activity. Symbols are sometimes used in the teachers' notes, however, and there is a chart at the end of the book with the symbols and guide words if you need to make reference to it. The symbols used in the book are those typically found in British-published material, but there is also and American version of the vowel chart for comparison if you are more accustomed to those symbols.

What are the other books in the PronPack collection?

The other books in the collection are:

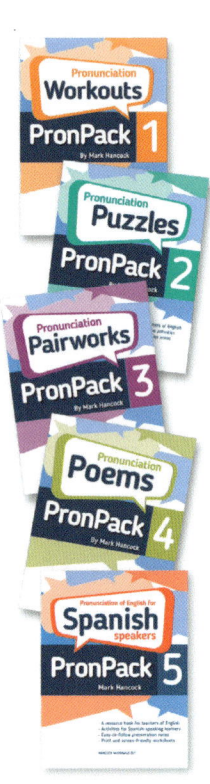

PronPack 1: Pronunciation Workouts: extended choral drill activities

PronPack 2: Pronunciation Puzzles: puzzles and game-like activities

PronPack 3: Pronunciation Pairworks: communication activities

PronPack 4: Pronunciation Poems: poems, raps and chants

PronPack 5: Pronunciation of English for Spanish Speakers: mixture of activity types

Contact us

We'd welcome your feedback on *www.pronpack.com* and if you have bought the eBook or Print version online we welcome your comments on the seller's website.

We look forward to hearing from you if you have any questions, ideas or suggestions.

Connect with us on:

twitter.com/pronpackbooks (@pronpackbooks)

facebook.com/pronpack

Kim and Tim

6.1

TEACHING FOCUS

Nasal consonants /m/, /n/, and /ŋ/ at the end of words

MINIMUM LEVEL

Pre-Intermediate

ACTIVITY

Rap and Map

WORKSHEETS

Print *Worksheet 6.1* for each student in the class.

AUDIO FILES

Audio 6.1-1

Audio 6.1-2

Background

The nasal consonants /m/, /n/, and /ŋ/ are formed when the air stream comes out of the nose rather than the mouth. The mouth position for /m/ is similar to /p/, /n/ is similar to /t/, and /ŋ/ is similar to /k/. The phonemes /m/ and /n/ sound very similar whether they are at the beginning or end of a word (although /n/ may sound like /m/ before a /p/ or /b/, or like an /ŋ/ before /k/ and /g/ – this change is known as assimilation.

Language Comparison

In Brazilian Portuguese, /m/ and /n/ don't occur at the end of words. Instead, the vowel is strongly nasalized. To English-speaker's ears, this sounds like a vowel followed by /ŋ/. So, for example, Portuguese *sim* (yes) sounds like English *sing*. As a result, words like *sun, sum* and *sung* all tend to sound the same in the speech of Brazilian learners.

Make sure that students are aware that these sound different in English. In the case of /m/, insist that your students close their lips completely at the end of words like *Kim, gym* and *ham*. They can check by looking at themselves in a mirror, or the cameras on their phones.

In the case of /n/, get students to think of how that sound is pronounced at the beginning of a word like *no* (the tip of the tongue touches the roof of the mouth behind the top teeth). Then tell them to make sure the same happens at the end of words like *sin*.

Rap Activity

1. Give out *Worksheet 6.1*. Read out the rhyme and check understanding (*have a fling* = have a short relationship). Alternatively, you can use *Audio 6.1-1* (or *Audio 6.1-2*, which is the backing music without the voice).

2. Say each line and ask the class to repeat it. Listen and check their pronunciation, especially to the sounds /m/, /n/, and /ŋ/ at the ends of words (shown in green). Notice that in *a man called Dan*, the /n/ of *man* changes to /ŋ/ because of the consonant /k/ which follows – see the explanation above. In all other cases, make sure the /m/ and /n/ are not pronounced like /ŋ/.

3. Say each pair of lines and ask the class to repeat them.

4. Get the whole class in chorus to say the poem together, making sure their lips close every time there is a letter *m*.

Map Activity

1. Ask the class to look at the map on the worksheet. Say pairs of words and ask them to identify the city, for example:
   You: *run, thing!*   **Class**: *Vitoria!*

   Note: In the resources on *pronpack.com*, you will find another version of this worksheet featuring a map of Europe instead of Brazil and neighbouring countries.

2. Ask student volunteers to call out words and the rest of the class to identify the city. If there are any mistakes, point out that they must be careful to distinguish the *n*, *m* and *ng* at the ends of the words.

3. Students work in pairs and do the same activity.

4. Students could extend the game by creating short 'tours', for example:

   Student A: *First go to run – sang, then go to rum – sam, after that, go to sum – Kim. And finally go to sum – king!*

   Student B: *Campo Grande, Santiago, La Paz, Barreiras!*

Kim had a **fling**
With a **guy** called **Tim**
She **met** him on a **swim**
At the **loc**al **gym**

Anne had a **plan**
With a **man** called **Dan**
To **drive** to Ja**pan**
In an **ice**-cream van

	Sam	**Kim**	**sang**	**thin**	**king**	**thing**
sun	Iquitos	Manaus	Santarem	Macapá	Belém	Fortaleza
sung	Pucallpa	Porto Velho	Alta Floresta	Marabá	Teresina	Maceió
sum	Arequipa	La Paz	Cuiabá	Brazília	Barreiras	Salvador
run	Iquique	Sucre	Campo Grande	São Paulo	Rio de Janeiro	Vitoria
rung	Antofagasta	Salta	Asunción	Curitiba	Santos	cruise ship
rum	Santiago	Córdoba	Buenos Aires	Porto Alegre	fishing boat	oil tanker

Rabbit in a Hat

6.2

TEACHING FOCUS

The phoneme /r/ at the beginning of words

MINIMUM LEVEL

Pre-Intermediate

ACTIVITY

Minimal pairs and rap

WORKSHEETS

Print *Worksheet 6.2* for each student in the class.

AUDIO FILES

Audio 6.2-1

Audio 6.2-2

Background

The sound of the phoneme /r/ varies quite a lot between different varieties of English. For some, the tip of the tongue is near the alveolar ridge, but curled back a little leaving a gap. For others, the tip of the tongue taps the alveolar ridge rapidly to create what is known as a 'rolled R'.

A different phoneme, /h/, is formed far down the throat, by narrowing the glottis so that air is forced through a narrow gap.

Language Comparison

At the beginning of words, many Brazilian speakers pronounce the /r/ in a way that sounds very like the English /h/, for example *rat* and *rabbit* sound like *hat* and *habit*. Students can usually correct this quite easily once they are aware of it, but often forget to do so.

Minimal Pair Activity

1. Give out *Worksheet 6.2*. Ask students to look at the photo and decide what the misunderstanding is. Answer: The person on the left pronounced *ride* with a sound like /h/ at the beginning. The person on the right thinks she said *hide*.

2. Ask students to look at the sentences **1 – 8**. Say each sentence twice, first with *Word **a*** and then with *Word **b***. Tell students to focus on the difference. Explain that if they pronounce *a* the same as *b*, people will not understand them correctly!

3. Say sentences at random, with either *Word* **a** or **b**. Tell students to identify which they hear – **a** or **b**.

4. Get volunteers from the class to do the same, saying sentences at random for their classmates to identify.

Rap Activity

1. Read out the poem (it has the form of a rap) and check understanding. Alternatively, you can use *Audio 6.2-1* (or *Audio 6.2-2*, which is the backing music without the voice). Students might ask for the meaning of *habit* (= *regular activity*).

2. Say each line and ask the class to repeat it. Listen and check their pronunciation, especially to the sounds /r/ and /h/ at the start of words (shown in red).

3. Say each pair of lines and ask the class to repeat them. Point out the linking symbols (shown in green). These show where the sound at the end of one word joins together with a vowel sound at the start of the next word.

4. Get the whole class in chorus to say the poem together, making sure the beat falls on the syllables in **bold**.

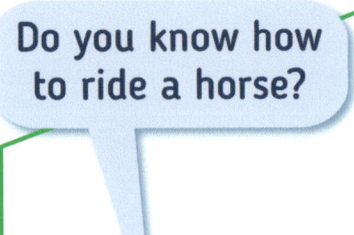

Do you know how to ride a horse?

Yeah, put it in the garage

1 Can you { a. ride / b. hide } a bike?

2 No { a. rats / b. hats } in the house please!

3 You'll need { a. rope / b. hope } to climb that mountain!

4 You can see that bird's { a. red / b. head }.

5 They { a. rung / b. hung } a bell in the church.

6 I know this type of lion's { a. rare / b. hair }.

7 The actor found a { a. role / b. hole } in the film.

8 My best friend's { a. Robby / b. hobby }.

If you see a **r**at
Hiding in a **h**at
If it's **big** like a **rabb**it
With **hab**its like a **rabb**it

Eyes bright **r**ed
Rabbit **ears** on its **head**
Per**haps** its **not** a **r**at
But a **rabb**it in a **h**at

6.3

Better Call Paul

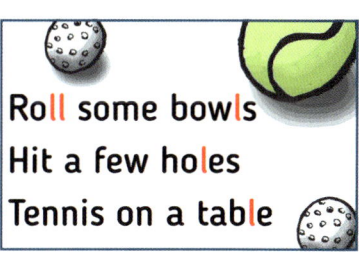

Roll some bowls
Hit a few holes
Tennis on a table

TEACHING FOCUS

The phoneme /l/ at the end of words

MINIMUM LEVEL

Pre-Intermediate

ACTIVITY

Minimal pairs and rap

WORKSHEETS

Print *Worksheet 6.3* for each student in the class.

AUDIO FILES

Audio 6.3–1

Audio 6.3–2

Background

The sound of the phoneme /l/ is different at the beginning or end of a syllable. At the beginning, it is clear, while at the end, it takes on some of the character of the vowel – this is known as the 'dark L'. In some accents, this process goes so far that the /l/ is no longer a consonant, but becomes a vowel similar to /ʊ/. For example, *will* sounds like *wiw* in the speech of some Londoners.

Language Comparison

In most of Brazil, the /l/ phoneme becomes like the vowel /ʊ/ at the end of a word, so that the Portuguese words *mau* and *mal* become homophones. Although some native speakers of English do the same (see above), it is best that students are aware of this and avoid it if they can in English.

Rap Activity

1. Give out *Worksheet 6.3*. Ask students to look at the photo and decide what the misunderstanding is. Answer: The person on the left pronounced *Hal* with a sound like /ʊ/ at the end instead of /l/. The person on the right thinks she said *how*.

2. Ask students to say the word *like* and focus on the consonant at the beginning of it. Ask them to notice what their tongue is doing. Answer: The tip of the tongue makes contact with the roof of the mouth just behind the teeth.

3. Ask students to try saying the words *boil*, *feel* etc. (beneath the photo on Worksheet 6.3). Tell them to make sure that for the /l/ sound, the tip of their tongue makes contact with the roof of the mouth, just as it did in *like*.

4. Ask students to look at the *Find the words...* activity. Go through the first question with them. Point out that the phrase *why lie* doesn't make sense. It fact, it should be *while I*. The reason for this mistake is that *why lie* and *while I* sound exactly the same if you pronounce them correctly. This is because, unlike in writing, there is no gap between words in speech, and it is often difficult to know if a consonant sound is at the end of one word or the beginning of the next.

If they find it difficult to pronounce the /l/ in *while I*, students can simply say *why lie* instead, because it is easier to say the /l/ at the start of a word than at the end!

5. Ask students to find the mistakes in the rest of the sentences. The words below the photograph are clues that will help them to find the mistakes. If you need to give more clues, you could also write the following words on the board:

   lie, eggs, awful, east, earn, ends, own, eyes, eight.

6. Get students to practice pronouncing the sentences.

Answer Key

1 *why lie = while I;* **2** *boy legs = boil eggs;* **3** *fee lawful = feel awful;*
4 *say least = sail east;* **5** *he learn = he'll earn;* **6** *say lends = sale ends;*
7 *I alone = I'll own;* **8** *pay lies = pale eyes;* **9** *go late = goal eight*

Rap Activity

1. Read out the poem (it has the form of a rap) and check understanding. Alternatively, you can use **Audio 6.3–1** (or **Audio 6.3–2**, which is the backing music without the voice). Students might ask for the meaning of *'em* (= *a short form of* **them**).

2. Say each line and ask the class to repeat it. Listen and check their pronunciation, especially to the sound /l/ at the end of words (shown in red).

3. Say each pair of lines and ask the class to repeat them.

4. Get the whole class in chorus to say the poem together, making sure they pronounce the sound /l/ at the end of words.

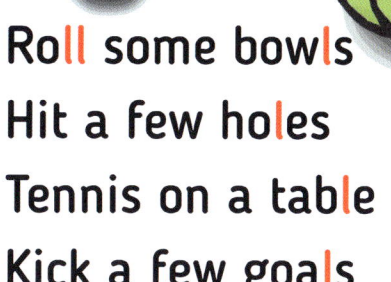

Better Call Paul
If you wanna play ball
Any kind of Ball
Paul's got 'em all

Roll some bowls
Hit a few holes
Tennis on a table
Kick a few goals

Play a little snooker
Gotta learn the rules
Or just stay cool
Playing Polo in the pool

^a**boil** ^b**feel** ^c**goal**

^d**he'll** ^e**I'll** ^f**pale**

^g**sail** ^h**sale** ⁱ**while**

Find the words above hidden in these sentences:

1 The phone rang why lie was in the shower.

2 She can't cook – she can't even boy legs!

3 Poor you – you must fee lawful!

4 After leaving the port, the boats say least.

5 When he's qualified, he learn a good salary.

6 Hurry to the shop – the say lends tomorrow!

7 When I've paid the bank, I alone my flat!

8 He had a long thin nose and strange pay lies.

9 The fans celebrated victory after go late.

Teas or Cheese?

6.4

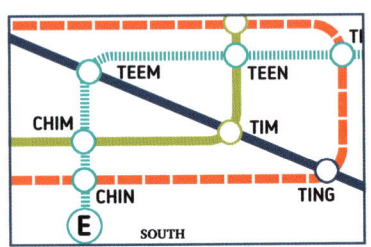

TEACHING FOCUS

When /t/ and /d/ become /tʃ/ and /dʒ/ before /i/

MINIMUM LEVEL

Pre-Intermediate

ACTIVITY

Rap and Guessing game

WORKSHEETS

Print **Worksheet 6.4** for each student in the class.

AUDIO FILES

Audio 6.4-1

Background

In English, the consonant phonemes /t/ and /d/ sound much the same before any vowel. They are distinct from the phonemes /tʃ/ and /dʒ/, making minimal pairs such as *teas* and *cheese*, or *deep* and *jeep*.

Language Comparison

Most Brazilian Portuguese speakers pronounce /t/ and /d/ differently when the following vowel is /i/, or at the end of a word. The phoneme /t/ sounds like /tʃ/ and /d/ sounds like /dʒ/. Students usually transfer this to English too, so that as *teas* becomes *cheese*, *beat* becomes *beach*, *deep* becomes *jeep* and *aid* becomes *age*. Although this is a difficult habit to break, it is important that students should do so – it can easily lead to misunderstandings.

Minimal Pair Activity

1. Give out *Worksheet 6.4*. Ask students to look at the photo and decide what the misunderstanding is. Answer: The customer pronounced *teas* with a sound like /tʃ/ at the beginning. The waiter thinks she said *cheese*.

2. Ask students to look at sentences **1 – 8**. Say each sentence twice, first with *Word* **a** and then with *Word* **b**. Tell students to focus on the difference. Explain that if they pronounce **a** the same as **b**, people will not understand them correctly!

3. Say sentences at random, with either *Word* **a** or **b**. Tell students to identify which they hear – **a** or **b**.

4. Get volunteers from the class to do the same, saying sentences at random for their classmates to identify.

Map Activity

1. Ask students to look at the metro map. Point out that the names of the stations in this city are all rather similar-sounding. They all contain consonant sounds featured in this lesson, as well as /iː/ or /ɪ/ (see **Lesson 10**), and final nasal consonant sounds (see **Lesson 1**).

2. Tell students to read the instructions below the map and answer the question (answer = *Chim*). If necessary, show them how this answer is reached, by holding up a copy of the map and following the route with a finger.

3. Tell the class to listen to you giving similar instructions, but change the names in each of the underlined gaps. For example:

*Get on the metro at **A** and go to **Teem**. Change lines and go to **Chin**. Change lines again and go one stop East. Where are you?*

Ask the class to listen very carefully and give you the answer (= ***Ting***).

Alternatively, you can use the four examples on *Audio 6.4-1* (**Answers:** 1 – *Tim*, 2 – *Cheem*, 3 – *Teen*, 4 – *Teen*).

4. Give a few more similar instructions to familiarize the class with the game. Then get a few volunteers to give instructions in a similar way. Tell them to pronounce the station names very carefully!

5. Get the students into pairs or small groups. Tell one student to give directions to a place. The others must listen and identify the place. Students take turns to be the speaker. If the listeners do not go to the intended station, get them to work out what went wrong.

6.4 Teas or Cheese?

What teas have you got?

Sorry, we don't have cheese...

1 We'd Like some { a. teas / b. cheese } please.

2 How many { a. tins / b. chins } have you got?

3 This is my friend { a. Dean / b. Gene }.

4 I think this game will end in { a. tears / b. cheers }.

5 I never leave { a. tips / b. chips } in restaurants.

6 I never tell people about my { a. aid / b. age }.

7 We { a. chained / b. change } our bikes outside.

8 We danced to the { a. beat / b. beach }.

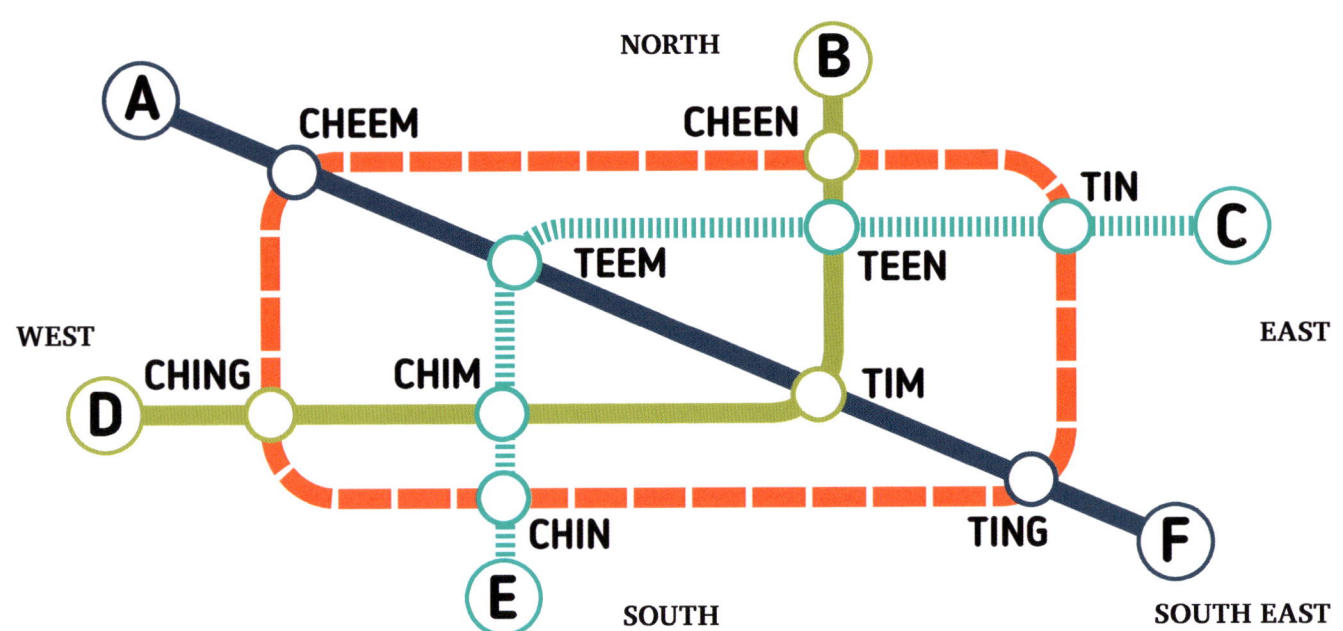

Get on the metro at __A__. Go to __TING__.
Change Lines and go to __CHIN__.
Change lines again and go one stop __NORTH__. **Where are you?**

6.5

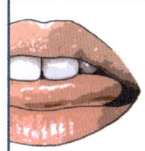

Thin might sou
Or *tin* sometim
Then may soun
Or *den* maybe
Try to say *TH*
Hard like *both*

n see the tip of
gue between the
in the standard

Background

The English phonemes /θ/ and /ð/ are produced with the tip of the tongue sticking out slightly between the teeth. The /θ/ is voiceless, as in *thin* and the /ð/ is voiced, as in *then*. However, there is a lot of variation in the pronunciation of these phonemes in different Englishes. For example, many speakers from England replace them with /f/ and /v/ so that *thin* sounds like *fin* and then sounds like *Venn*. Meanwhile, many speakers in Ireland and Jamaica replace them with /t/ and /d/ so that *thin* sounds like *tin* and *then* sounds like *den*. Many non-native speakers of English also use these alternatives, or a third possibility: many speakers from France and Germany, for example, replace them with /s/ and /z/ so that *thin* sounds like *sin* and *then* sounds like *zen*.

Language Comparison

Most Brazilian Portuguese learners have great difficulty with /θ/ and /ð/, no matter how much time their teachers spend on these sounds. Instead, students tend to use some of the alternative sounds mentioned above. In terms of intelligibility, it is probably fine for them to do so. These variations are so widespread that most listeners will have heard them before. However, it is definitely important for students to be aware of these sounds and their variations. You could take a flexible approach. Encourage your students to aim for /θ/ and /ð/, but if they continue to use alternatives such as /f/ and /v/, don't worry too much about it.

Rap Activity

1. Give out **Worksheet 6.5**. Read out the rhyme and check understanding (People may pronounce the TH sounds /θ/ and /ð/ in a variety of ways). Alternatively, you can use **Audio 6.5-1**.

2. Say each line and ask the class to repeat it. Listen and check pronunciation, especially to the sounds represented by the letters in green. Point out that in the standard pronunciation of the TH sounds, you can see the tip of the tongue between the teeth, as in the picture. The 'hard' sound /θ/ has no voicing (vibration in the throat) while the 'soft' sound /ð/ there *is* voicing (vibration in the throat).

3. Say each pair of lines and ask the class to repeat them.

4. Get the whole class in chorus to say the poem together.

Board Game Activity

Tell students in pairs or groups to look at the grid at the bottom of the page. Explain that the phrases are written as they are pronounced (like the words in the poem). Tell students to work together to identify the words which are spelt wrongly in the sentences and explain why. Do the first two or three as a whole class to get them started. For example: In **1**, *bat* should be spelt *bath*. The speaker has pronounced TH like /t/.

Alternatively, pairs or groups could do this activity as a dice game:

1. Students place a counter on the top arrow and take turns to throw the dice. They move their counter by that number of squares.

2. When they land on a square, students have to explain which word is wrongly spelt, and why.

3. If someone lands on a square where someone has already been, they have to make a different sentence using the word which was wrongly spelt.

4. The first student to get past Square **20** is the winner.

Answer Key

1 *bat = bath,* **2** *true = through,* **3** *fin = thin,* **4** *sick = thick,*
5 *deaf = death,* **6** *fought = thought,* **7** *free = three,* **8** *breed = breathe,*
9 *close = clothes,* **10** *turd = third,* **11** *tank = thank,* **12** *boat = both,*
13 *mats = maths,* **14** *sink = think,* **15** *sings = things,*
16 *sums = thumbs,* **17** *worse = worth,* **18** *norse = north,*
19 *bays = bathe,* **20** *tree = three*

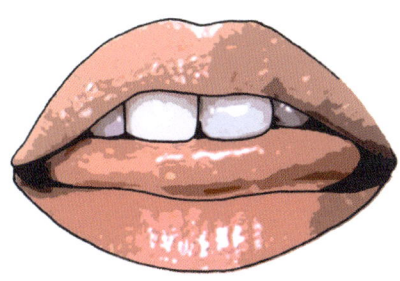

You can see the tip of the tongue between the teeth in the standard pronunciation of *TH*

*Th*in might sound like *f*in
Or *t*in sometimes *s*in

*Th*en may sound like *V*enn
Or *d*en maybe *z*en

Try to say *TH*
Hard like bo*th* or soft like o*th*er

But if you can't, don't worry
We'll understand each o*th*er

1 A shower or a bat?	**2** I looked true a telescope.	**3** Don't walk on fin ice!	**4** We wear sick coats in winter	**5** It's a matter of life or deaf!
10 It's the turd of August.	**9** She isn't wearing any close.	**8** There's no air, I can't breed!	**7** It's free oclock already!	**6** Have you ever fought about living abroad?
11 I'm writing to say tank you.	**12** Me and my wife are boat Irish.	**13** I hated mats at school.	**14** What do you sink of my new car?	**15** I packed my sings in my suitcase.
20 I've got tree sisters.	**19** It's too cold to sun bays.	**18** Manchester is norse of London.	**17** How much money is your house worse?	**16** I've got eight fingers and two sums.

Bear or Pear?

6.6

Make a puff of air

TEACHING FOCUS

The phonemes /p/, /t/ and /k/

MINIMUM LEVEL

Pre-Intermediate

ACTIVITY

Rap and minimal pair game

WORKSHEETS

Print *Worksheet 6.6* for each student in the class.

AUDIO FILES

Audio 6.6-1

Audio 6.6-2

Background

The English phonemes /p/, /t/ and /k/, when they occur at the beginning of a word, are usually pronounced with a puff of air from the mouth. This is one of the things which helps to distinguish them from /b/, /d/ and /g/ (along with the voicing difference). You can test for this by holding a piece of tissue paper suspended in front of your mouth. When you say *pear*, the puff of air will hit the paper and make it move. When you say *bear*, the paper will remain still. However, this puff of air is not present in all varieties of English. For example, it is not noticeable in the English of many Indian speakers. Also, it is not present in all contexts. For example, there is no puff of air when /p/, /t/ and /k/ are in a consonant cluster such as *spring*, and not usually at the end of a word.

Language Comparison

Although Brazilian Portuguese has the three phonemes /p/, /t/ and /k/, they are not pronounced with a puff of air. Compare the sound of the Portuguese word *pai* and English *pie*. They are almost homophones, except for the presence of a puff of air in the English word. Absence of a puff of air can make /p/, /t/ and /k/ easily confused with /b/, /d/ and /g/ when Brazilian learners speak English, so that *pie* sounds rather like *buy*, for example.

Rap Activity

1. Give out *Worksheet 6.6*. Read out the rhyme and check understanding (*puff* = a strong breath outwards – see the cartoon illustration). Alternatively, you can use *Audio 6.6-1*. Ask students to find the words in the poem for the things in the picture.

2. Demonstrate the puff of air. Say *pear* with a piece of paper (tissue paper is even better) in front of your mouth. Show how the paper is moved by your breath after the sound /p/. Repeat the experiment with *bear* and show how the paper does not move.

3. Say each line and ask the class to repeat it. Listen and check their pronunciation of the phonemes /p/, /t/ and /k/.

4. Say each pair of lines and ask the class to repeat them.

5. Get the whole class in chorus to say the poem together.

Minimal Pair Game

1. Demonstrate how the Pinball diagram works. Tell your students to place their fingers on the number one. Explain that if you say 'A', they must move downward to the left, and if you say 'B', they must move downwards to the right

2. Say **1** – *Left;* **2** – *Left;* **3** – *Right;* **4** – *Left.* Ask the students which shape they have reached (answer = *bell*). Repeat this with other sequences to reach the other shapes until you are sure students have understood the idea of the game.

3. Demonstrate the game. Tell students you will say words, randomly chosen either from **Left** e.g. *peach* or from **Right** e.g. *beach*. Explain that they should follow the path on the Pinball diagram just as they did in *Step 2*. For example:

   You: 1 – *beach,* **2** – *bear,* **3** – *pie,* **4** – *big*
   Students: *Cherries!*

4. Say four words (or play *Audio 6.6–2*), and check that the students have all reached the intended shape (star, bell, lemon, cherries or diamond). Repeat this step a few times (there are 3 different paths on *Audio 6.6–2* . **Answers: 1** – *cherries,* **2** – *diamond,* **3** – *lemon*).

5. Tell students to practice in pairs or small groups taking turns to speak and listen. One student says the words and the other or others listen and follow the route on the Pinball diagram.

   The objective is for all of the listeners to reach the shape the speaker intended. If they fail, the speaker must try again and exaggerate the difference more.

Make a puff of air
For a peach or a pear
But no puff's there
For a beach or a bear

 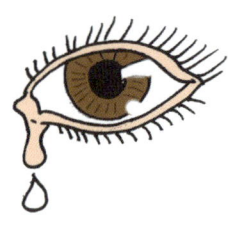

There's a puff you hear
In a coat or a tear
But non you can hear
In a goat or a deer

 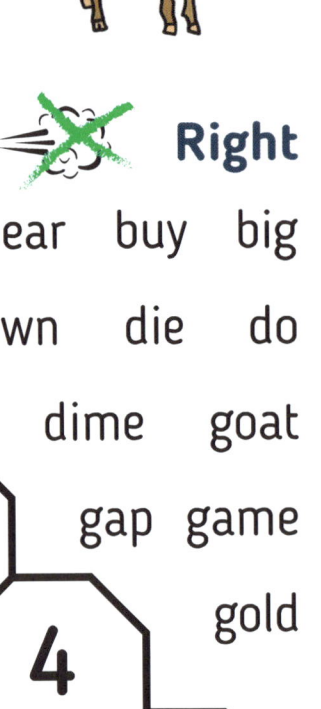

Left 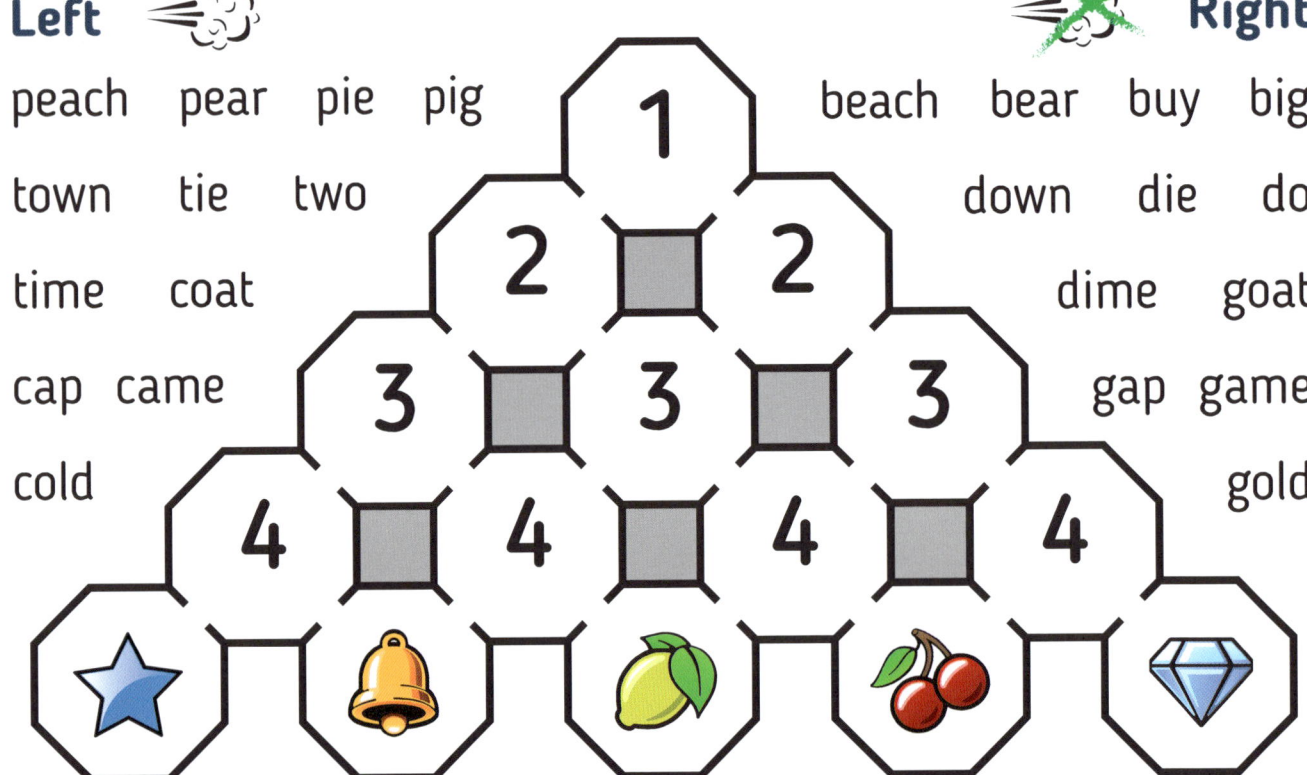 **Right**

peach	pear	pie	pig	**1**	beach	bear	buy	big
town	tie	two		**2** **2**	down	die	do
time	coat		**3** **3** **3**	dime	goat
cap	came		**4** **4** **4** **4**	gap	game
cold			gold

Piece or Peas?

6.7

> Would you like some peas with that?

TEACHING FOCUS

The phonemes /s/ and /z/ at the end of words

MINIMUM LEVEL

Pre-Intermediate

ACTIVITY

Minimal Pairs and map

WORKSHEETS

Print **Worksheet 6.7** for each student in the class.

AUDIO FILES

Audio 6.7-1

Background

The English phonemes /s/ and /z/ can be difficult to distinguish at the end of a word, and yet because of –s endings (plurals, possessives, verb inflections), they often occur in word-final position, and the choice of /s/ or /z/ often creates a difference in meaning – for example, *peace* or *peas*. The two sounds are similar, but the first is voiceless and the second is voiced. You can feel a vibration in the throat for /z/ but not for /s/. However, this may be difficult to hear, so you could also point out to learners a second difference between them: a vowel sound before /s/ is pronounced shorter than before /z/. Vowel sounds are *clipped* before voiceless consonants, and this may be easier to say and hear than the voicing difference.

Language Comparison

Although Brazilian Portuguese has the phonemes /s/ and /z/, there are often problems. One problem relates to grammatical endings for plurals, possessives and verb inflections. These are always written with the letter S, but it may correspond to /s/ or /z/.

The letter S may also correspond to /s/ or /z/ in Portuguese, but the patterns are different. For example, /z/ doesn't occur at the end of words. Meanwhile, an S between vowels will be /z/ in Portuguese, and if learners carry this over into their English, they will say *buzzes* instead of *buses*. Another example is in consonant clusters, where the S is pronounced /z/ before the consonants /m/, /n/, /l/ and /r/. As a result, the Portuguese word *smoking* sounds like *izmoking*.

Minimal Pair Activity

1. Give out **Worksheet 6.7**. Ask students to look at the photo and decide what the misunderstanding is. Answer: The waiter pronounced *peas* with a sound like /s/ at the end. The customer thinks she said *piece*.

2. Explain the difference in pronunciation between *peas* and *piece*. *Peas* ends with a /z/ sound – you can feel vibration if you put your hand on your throat. *Piece* ends with a /s/ sound – there is no vibration. Also point out that the vowel sounds shorter in *piece* than *peas*

3. Ask students to look at the sentences **1 - 12**. Say some of the sentences twice, first with option **a** and then with option **b**.

Tell students to focus on the difference. Explain that if they pronounce **a** the same as **b**, people will not understand them correctly!

4. Say sentences at random, with either option *a* or *b*. Tell students to identify which they hear – **a** or **b**. Alternatively, you can use *Audio 6.7-1* for this activity (**Answers: 1 – a, 2 – b, 3 – b, 4 – a, 5 – b, 6 – a, 7- b, 8 – a, 9 – b, 10 – a, 11 – a, 12 – a**).

5. Get volunteers from the class to do the same, saying sentences at random for their classmates to identify.

Maze Activity

1. Ask students to look at the maze at the bottom of the page. Explain that the objective is to find routes from the /s/ and /z/ symbols at the top corners to the matching symbols at the bottom corners.

2. Explain that they can go from any room to a neighbouring room with a connecting door or corridor. On the route from /s/ to /s/, you can only pass through a room if the phrase contains that sound. On the route from /z/ to /z/, you can only pass through a room if the phrase contains that sound.

3. As an example, work through the first two rooms for the sound /s/ as a whole class (Answer with the sound underlined: *go* **s***low. a new* **s***port*). Notice that some neighbouring rooms do not have a door between them. You can't go directly from top left /s/ to *a new sport*, for example, because there is no door.

4. Ask students to do the same for the remaining routes. Advise them to use different coloured pens or pencils to mark each route if possible.

5. Check the answers together.

6. Go through the routes again, pronouncing all of the phrases and getting the class to repeat. Point out some interesting contrasts:

   close to home has /s/ but *close the door* has /z/; *no excuse* has /s/ but *excuse me* has /z/; *wife's name* has /s/ but *wives leave* has /z/; *cat's* has /s/ but *dog's* has /z/, *a lost tooth* has /s/ but *lose a tooth* has /z/.

Answer Key

/s/ – go slow, a new sport, a lost tooth, close to home, no excuse, a cat's eye, an east wind, a box of books, Kate's flat, my wife's name, no smoking – /s/

/z/ – your wives leave, an easy game, Ben's flat, excuse me, close the door, a dog's eyes, lose a tooth, a news report – /z/

Would you like some peas with that?

Piece of what?

1 I found some
{ a. peace
  b. peas } in the garden.

2 That
{ a. price
  b. prize } looks fantastic!

3 Your
{ a. niece
  b. knees } must be tired.

4 We need five
{ a. pence
  b. pens } more.

5 What makes
{ a. ice
  b. eyes } blue or brown?

6 That
{ a. place
  b. play's } made me sad.

7 What causes the price
{ a. rice is
  b. rises } ?

8 { a. Dance moves
  b. Dan's moves } are cool!

9 What makes the
{ a. car slow
  b. cars low } ?

10 Anne's
{ a. slips
  b. lips } are blue.

11 I've never seen
{ a. June snows
  b. June's nose } !

12 { a. She smiles
  b. She's miles } from the window.

S	go slow	an east wind	a box of books	**Z**
	a new sport	a cat's eye	an easy game	your wives leave
a news report	lose a tooth	a dog's eyes	Kate's flat	my wife's name
	lost a tooth	no excuse	Ben's flat	no smoking
Z	close to home	close the door	excuse me	**S**

Smart Bart

6.8

TEACHING FOCUS
Initial consonant clusters with /s/

MINIMUM LEVEL
Pre-Intermediate

ACTIVITY
Listening maze and minimal pairs

WORKSHEETS
Print **Worksheet 6.8** for each student in the class.

AUDIO FILES
No audio with this activity

Audio 6.8–1

Background

Different languages have different 'rules' about which consonant clusters are 'allowed' at the beginning of syllables. In English, there are many clusters with /s/ followed by one or two more consonants, for example *slow*, *small*, *sport* and *strict*. These combinations do not exist in many languages and may cause difficulty.

Language Comparison

When English words with an initial consonant cluster such as *sport* have a cognate in Brazilian Portuguese, there is often an initial vowel in the spelling and pronunciation, for example, *esporte*. So perhaps it's not surprising that Brazilian learners often insert such a vowel before /s/ clusters in English. It is worth making students aware of this.

The simple addition of a vowel before /s/ clusters may not be problematic for intelligibility. However, in addition to this issue, students may change the /s/ to /z/ when the following consonant is /m/, /n/, /l/ or /r/, so that *slow* may sound like *izlow*. The combination of added vowel *plus* changed consonant can make the student's speech less intelligible.

Listening Activity

1. Give out **Worksheet 6.8**. Ask students to look at the people in the video meeting. They all have nicknames including a descriptive word beginning with S – for example *Slim Kim*. You may need to help learners with some of the descriptive words:
   scruffy = someone whose appearance is untidy;
   slob = someone who is lazy and careless, and not very active.
   Note that *smart* has two meanings: clever, and well-dressed.

2. Explain that students must listen and number the people in the video meeting in the order they are mentioned. Number one is already given as an example. Read out the rhyme, or play **Audio 6.8–1**.
   Answers: 1 *Slim Kim*, **2** *Sport Rory*, **3** *Smart Bart*, **4** *Stylish Eilish*, **5** *Bob the Slob*, **6** *Small Paul*, **7** *Smiley Miley*, **8** *Scruffy Duffy*, **9** *Slow Jo*.

3. Ask students to listen again and try to write what the people say. They all say one word only. The first answer is given as an example.
   Answer Key: see audio script on next page.

Audio script:

> Slim Kim said, 'Hello!'
> And Sporty Rory said, 'Go!'
>
> Smart Bart said, 'Who?'
> And Stylish Eilish said, 'You!'
>
> Bob the Slob said, 'No!'
> And Small Paul said, 'Oh!'
>
> Smiley Miley said, 'Great!'
> And Scruffy Duffy said, 'Wait!'
>
> Slow Jo said, 'Hi!'
> And everyone else said 'Bye!'

4. Go through the answers together. Drill the pronunciation of each description. Notice that most of them rhyme, e.g. *Slim Kim*.

5. Ask the students to repeat the rhyme after you or the audio, two lines at a time. Check students' pronunciation of the /s/ at the beginning of the adjectives. There are two possible problems:
   1. They may replace /s/ with /z/, especially in the adjectives beginning *sm* and *sl*.
   2. They may add an extra vowel sound in front of the /s/ of each adjective.

Minimal Pair Activity

1. Ask students to look at **1**. Say *sentence* **a** and then *sentence* **b**. Then say them again, but only the beginning of each sentence and stopping before the part in grey. Point out that the two sentence beginnings are almost the same, but there is an extra vowel (the *a*) before the adjective in **b**. Notice also that the possessive 's after each name blends together with the s at the beginning of each adjective, so it sounds like a single /s/.

2. For each of **1 – 7**, say one sentence beginning at random, either **a** or **b**. Tell students to identify which they hear – **a** or **b**.

3. Get volunteers from the class to do the same, saying sentences at random for their classmates to identify. Monitor the activity. Notice that if students make the mistake of adding an extra vowel syllable before all the s the adjectives, they will not be able to distinguish **a** from **b**!

4. Ask students to do the activity in pairs, taking turns to speak and listen. The speaker says one of the sentence beginnings. The listener should complete the sentence. For example:

   Student A: Kim's a slim …
   Student B: young woman!

1 a. Kim's slim ... and healthy.
   b. Kim's a slim ... young woman.

2 a. Bart's smart ... and quick.
   b. Bart's a smart ... young man.

3 a. Rory's sporty ... and fit.
   b. Rory's a sporty ... type of guy.

4 a. Jo's slow ... and moody.
   b. Jo's a slow ... moving girl.

5 a. Paul's small ... and timid.
   b. Paul's a small ... boy.

6 a. Duffy's scruffy ... and careless.
   b. Duffy's a scruffy ... kind of girl.

7 a. Eilish is stylish ... and trendy.
   b. Eilish is a stylish ... person.

6.9

Cough or Coffee?

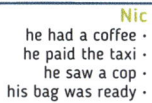

Nic
he had a coffee ·
he paid the taxi ·
he saw a cop ·
his bag was ready ·

Jackie
· her bag was red
· she wanted a cook
· she paid the tax
· she read the notes

TEACHING FOCUS

Adding a vowel or reducing a vowel at the end of words

MINIMUM LEVEL

Pre-Intermediate

ACTIVITY

Minimal pairs and question and answer game

WORKSHEETS

Print *Worksheet 6.9* for each student in the class.

AUDIO FILES

Audio 6.9-1 ▮▮ ↺

Background

You can find all of the consonant phonemes at the end of English words except /h/, /w/ and /j/.

Language Comparison

In Portuguese, most words end with a vowel sound and very few consonant sounds are 'allowed' at the end of a word. Perhaps for this reason, Brazilian learners tend to add a vowel after final consonants in English. So, for example, they may add an /i/ at the end of *cough*, making it sound like *coffee*.

However, there is another feature of Portuguese which confuses the issue even further. The /i/ vowel at the end of a word tends to be reduced so that it is sometimes difficult to hear. As a result, *coffee* may sound like *cough*. These two characteristics of Brazilian learner English can lead to misunderstandings. The second characteristic is perhaps more serious than the first in terms of intelligibility, since cutting sounds is more problematic than adding them.

Minimal Pairs Activity

1. Give out *Worksheet 6.9*. Ask students to look at the photo and decide what the misunderstanding is. Answer: The doctor intended to say *cough*, but the patient thought she said *coffee*.

2. Ask students to look at the sentences **1 - 10**. Say each sentence twice (or the first few of them, at least), first with *Word* **a** and then with *Word* **b**. Tell students to focus on the difference. Explain that if they pronounce **a** the same as **b**, people will not understand them correctly. For *Word* **a**, they should make sure they don't add an extra vowel sound at the end. For *Word* **b**, they should make sure they pronounce the final vowel sound loud and clear!

3. Say sentences at random, with either *Word* **a** or *Word* **b**. Tell students to identify which they hear – **a** or **b**. Alternatively, you can use *Audio 6.9-1* for this activity (**Answers**: 1 – **b**, 2 – **a**, 3 – **a**, 4 – **a**, 5 – **b**, 6 – **b**, 7– **a**, 8 – **b**, 9 – **a**, 10 – **a**).

4. Get volunteers from the class to do the same, saying sentences at random for their classmates to identify.

© Mark Hancock 2021   PronPack 6 Pronunciation for Brazilian learners: 6.9 Cough or Coffee?   33

Question and Answer Game

1. Ask students to look at the pictures of **Jack, Jackie, Nic** and **Nicky**. Point out that their names are similar. However, the names of the two men have one syllable and the names of the two women have two – there's an extra vowel sound at the end. Say some of the names a few times at random and ask students to say *the man* or *the woman*. For example:

   You: *Nicky*

   Students: *The woman!*

2. Ask students to look at the information below each picture. They should cover up the questions below (although don't worry too much if some of them want to look). Now read out the questions – but randomly, not in the order they are printed. Ask students to listen and answer. Notice that the questions are in similar-sounding pairs, so students must listen very carefully! Example:

   You: *Who had eighty dollars?*

   Students: *Nicky!*

3. Ask volunteers from the class to say some of the questions for their classmates to answer. Remind them to be careful with the word endings – don't add a vowel to words which end in a consonant like cough, and if a word ends in a vowel, be sure to pronounce it clearly.

4. Get students to play the game in pairs. After a while, if they want to make the activity more challenging, the student who is listening could turn the page over and try to answer the questions from memory!

Have you had a cough?

No, I had a cup of tea.

Jack

- he had a cough
- he had eight dollars
- he saw a copy
- he loved Kung Fu moves

Nic

- he had a coffee
- he paid the taxi
- he saw a cop
- his bag was ready

Jackie
- her bag was red
- she wanted a cook
- she paid the tax
- she read the notes

Nicky

- she had a eighty dollars
- she read the notice
- she loved Kung Fu movies
- she wanted a cookie

1 The { a. cough / b. coffee } was awful!

2 The { a. tax / b. taxi } was expensive.

3 I got the job – it's { a. part-time / b. party time }!

4 That { a. cook / b. cookie } was the best!

5 It's { a. eight / b. eighty } days till Christmas!

6 I've seen that Kung Fu { a. move / b. movie } before.

7 Pick the fruit when its { a. red / b. ready } .

8 I prefer fruit when its { a. juice / b. juicy } .

9 Do you know { a. Jack / b. Jackie } Brown?

10 I didn't take any { a. notes / b. notice } .

Who...
had a cough?	Jack
had a coffee?	Nic
had eight dollars?	Jack
had eighty dollars?	Nicky
paid the tax?	Jackie
paid the taxi?	Nic
read the notes?	Jackie
read the notice?	Nicky
saw a cop?	Nic
saw a copy?	Jack
loved Kung Fu moves?	Jack
loved Kung Fu movies?	Nicky
wanted a cook?	Jackie
wanted a cookie?	Nicky

Whose...
bag was red?	Jackie
bag was ready?	Nic

Live or Leave?

6.10

Background

In English, there is a contrast between the vowel phoneme /ɪ/ (for example, in *sit*) and the vowel phoneme /iː/ (for example, in *seat*). The first is shorter, with the muscles relaxed. The second is longer (the /ː/ part of the symbol means *long*), with the muscles around the mouth tense. There are quite a lot of words which are distinguished by this vowel difference alone, so it is quite important. There are also some potentially embarrassing words with this distinction (*shit* and *sheet*; *piss* and *piece*)!

Language Comparison

In Portuguese, there is only one vowel phoneme in the same area as /ɪ/ and /iː/. It is represented with the symbol /i/. As you can see, it is like the vowel in seat, but not long. There is no vowel sound like /ɪ/ in Portuguese so this is likely to cause difficulty. Point out that /ɪ/ needs to be short, but also with a very relaxed face, not smiley like /iː/.

Minimal Pair Activity

1. Give out *Worksheet 6.10* Ask students to look at the photo and decide what the misunderstanding is.

   Answer: The person on the left pronounced *live* with a sound like /iː/ in the middle. The person on the right thinks she said *leave*.

2. Ask students to look at the sentences **1 - 8**. Say each sentence twice, first with *Word* **a** and then with *Word* **b**. Tell students to focus on the difference. Explain that if they pronounce **a** the same as **b**, people will not understand them correctly!

3. Say sentences at random, with either *Word* **a** or **b**. Tell students to identify which they hear – **a** or **b**.

4. Get volunteers from the class to do the same, saying sentences at random for their classmates to identify.

Rap Activity

1. Read out the poem (it has the form of a rap) and check understanding. Alternatively, you can use *Audio 6.10–1* (or *Audio 6.10–2*, which is the backing music without the voice). Students could ask for the meaning of *gotta* (= *have got to*).

2. Say each line and ask the class to repeat it. Listen and check their pronunciation, especially to the sounds /ɪ/ and /iː/ (shown in red).

3. Say each pair of lines and ask the class to repeat them. Point out that the beat falls on the words/syllables in **bold**.

4. Get the whole class in chorus to say the poem together, making sure the beat falls on the syllables in bold.

Would you like to live here?

Leave? No I love it here

1 I'd like to { a. live / b. leave } here.

2 Can you { a. fill / b. feel } the gap?

3 What's in the { a. bins / b. beans }?

4 I don't like high { a. hills / b. heels }.

5 I can see { a. you're fit / b. your feet }.

6 There's a { a. ship / b. sheep } in the river!

7 The sun's { a. hitting / b. heating } my face.

8 That's the { a. list / b. least } of our problems.

Don't just **sit**
With **sli**ppers on your **feet**
Listen to the **mus**ic
Dance to the **beat**

Dance to the beat!

Don't just **sit** there
Eating **chips**
Get up off your **seat**
And **move** those **hips**

Dance and **sing**
It'll **make** you f**ee**l **fit**
Be**fore** we all **leave**
Gotta **live** a little **bit**!

Brad or Bread?

6.11

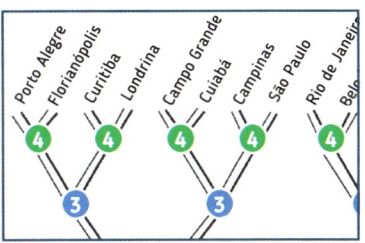

TEACHING FOCUS

Distinguishing /æ/ and /e/

MINIMUM LEVEL

Pre-Intermediate

ACTIVITY

Rap and minimal pair game

WORKSHEETS

Print one copy of **Worksheet 6.11** for each student in the class.

AUDIO FILES

Audio 6.11-1 ⏸ ↺

Audio 6.11-2 ⏸ ↺

Audio 6.11-3 ⏸ ↺

Background

The English phonemes /æ/ and /e/distinguish pairs of words such as *mat* and *met*. For /æ/, the jaw is more open than for /e/, but the exact sounds vary across different accents. For example, in Australia and New Zealand, the /æ/ is less open than in the UK and the US, so that *mat* sounds like UK *met*. However, in Australia and New Zealand the two words can still be distinguished, because the /e/ sound is also more closed. This reminds us of an important fact in pronunciation teaching: with phonemes, what is important is not the exact sound quality of the phonemes, but rather the fact that they must be distinguishable from each other.

Language Comparison

For Brazilian learners, the vowel phoneme /e/ is not problematic, as there is an equivalent in Portuguese. However, there is no /æ/, and students often produce a sound like /e/ instead, so that pairs like *mat* and *met* are indistinguishable. Advise students to open their jaw much wider for the vowel in *mat*. They can check this by putting their thumb on their chin and finger on their nose. When they say *met* followed by *mat*, the finger and thumb should move apart!

Rap Activity

1. Give out **Worksheet 6.11**. Ask students to look at the photo and decide what the misunderstanding is.
   Answer: The child pronounced *Brad* with a sound like /e/ in the middle. The baker thinks she said *bread*.

2. Read out the poem (it has the form of a limerick) and check understanding. Alternatively, you can use **Audio 6.11-1**, (or **Audio 6.11-2**, which is the backing music without the voice).

3. Say each line and ask the class to repeat it. Listen and check their pronunciation, especially the sounds /æ/ and /e/ (shown in green).

4. Say each line and ask the class to repeat it. Point out that the beat falls on the words/syllables in **bold**.

5. Get the whole class in chorus to say the poem together, making sure the beat falls on the syllables in **bold**.

Minimal Pair Game

1. Ask students to look at the sentences **1 – 4** in **Set 1** at the bottom of the page. Say each sentence twice, first with *Word **a*** and then with *Word **b***. Tell students to focus on the difference. Explain that if they pronounce **a** the same as **b**, people will not understand them correctly!

2. Say sentences at random, with either *Word **a*** or **b**. Tell students to identify which they hear – **a** or **b**.

3. Get volunteers from the class to do the same, saying sentences at random for their classmates to identify.

4. Now ask students to look at the diagram of routes to cities around the world. Tell them to put their finger on the *number **1***. Explain that if they hear a sentence with *Word **a*** they should move to the *number **2*** on the left, and if they hear *Word **b*** they should move to the *number **2*** on the right.

   Alternatively, you could use **Audio 6.11-3**, which has one path for each set (**Answers: Set 1** = *Fortaleza*, **Set 2** = *Curitiba*).

5. Now read out *Sentence **1*** from **Set 1** with either *Word **a*** or *Word **b***, and the students move their finger accordingly. Then repeat this process with *Sentences **2 – 4*** until students reach one of the destinations at the top. For example:

   You: 1 – *Could I borrow a pan*, **2** – *I saw the men arrive*,
       3 - *It's not that bed is it?*, **4** – *I'm looking for Brad*.

   Students: *Campinas!*

6. If students went to a different city from the one you intended, try to find out what went wrong. Then play the game a few more times.

7. Get students to play the game in pairs or small groups, with one saying the sentences and the other(s) moving their finger to a destination. They can use the sentences from **Set 2** as well.

A **fun**ny young **man** called **Brad**
Pro**nounced** his **name** like '**bread**'
Brad had a **cat**
Its **name** was **Pat**
But he **called** it '**Pet**' in**stead**!

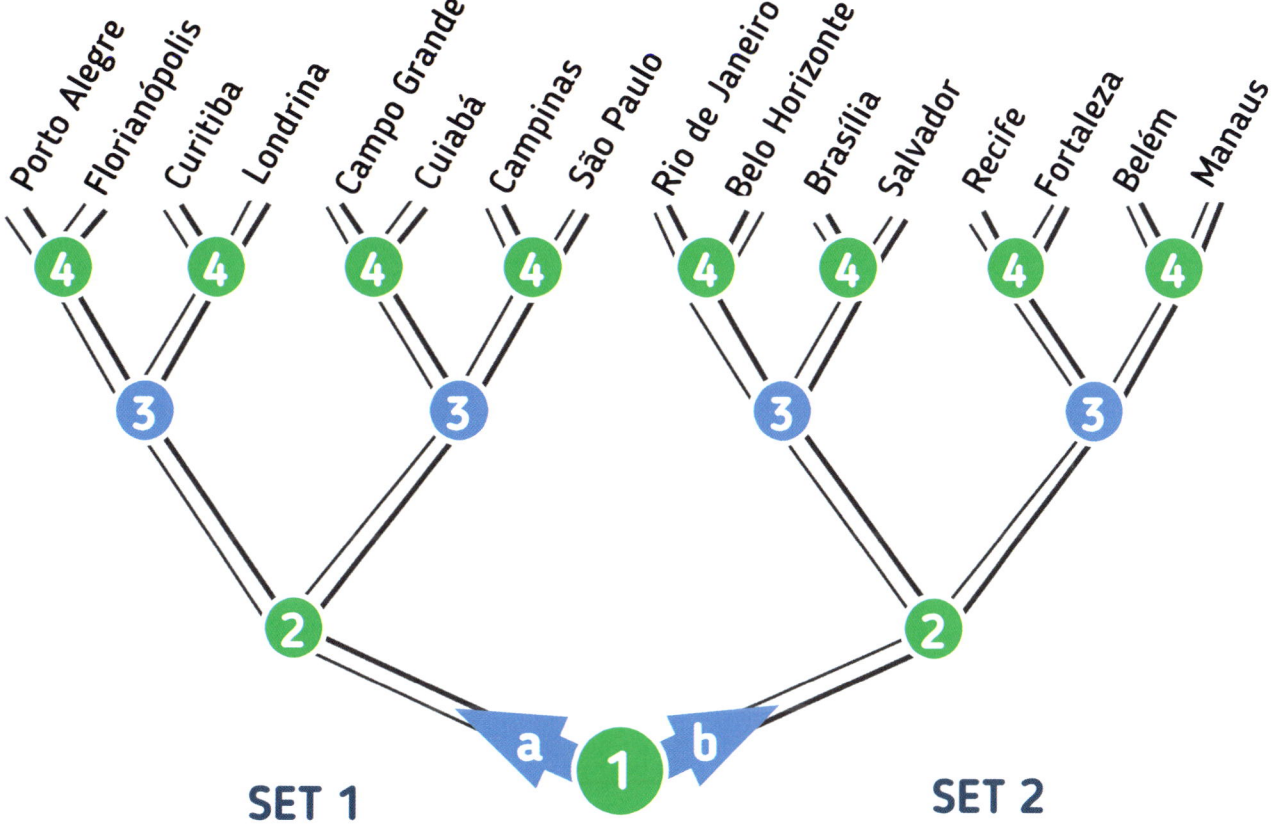

SET 1

1 Could I borrow a { a. pan / b. pen } ?

2 I saw the { a. man / b. men } arrive.

3 It's not that { a. bad / b. bed } is it?

4 I'm looking for { a. Brad / b. bread } .

SET 2

1 We went on a { a. track / b. trek } in the jungle.

2 That's where the { a. son sat / b. sun set } .

3 Your { a. gas / b. guess } is as good as mine.

4 I saw a { a. band / b. bend } in the road.

River of Vowels

6.12

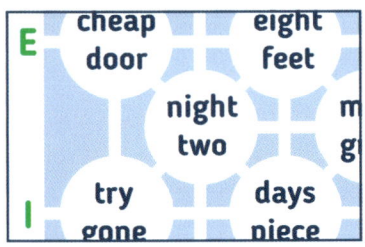

TEACHING FOCUS
Spelling and pronunciation of the alphabet vowels

MINIMUM LEVEL
Pre-Intermediate

ACTIVITY
Rap and Maze

WORKSHEETS
Print **Worksheet 6.12** for each student in the class.

AUDIO FILES

Audio 6.12-1

Audio 6.12-2

Background

English has only five vowel letters but as many as 20 vowel sounds (depending on the accent). So the five letters have to be used creatively in order to represent so many phonemes. In addition, the language has various influences such as French, German, Latin and Greek, each with its own spelling conventions. The result is that English spelling is complex, and especially the vowels. This lesson focuses on the sounds of the five vowel letters as they are pronounced in the alphabet - /eɪ, iː, aɪ, əʊ and (j)uː/ and the various alternative spellings of those five sounds.

Language Comparison

Like English, Portuguese has five vowel letters. However, it has fewer vowel sounds, and the relationship of spelling to pronunciation is much more straightforward. As a result, students often find the connection of English spelling to pronunciation very difficult and frustrating.

Rap Activity

1. Give out **Worksheet 6.12**. Read out the poem on the left of the worksheet (it has the form of a rap) and check understanding. Alternatively, you can use **Audio 6.12-1** (or **Audio 6.12-2**, which is the backing music without the voice).

2. Say each line and ask the class to repeat it. Listen and check their pronunciation, especially to the sounds of the vowel letters as pronounced in the alphabet.

3. Say each pair of lines and ask the class to repeat them.

4. Get the whole class in chorus to say the poem together.

Maze Activity

1. Ask students to look at the maze. Explain that the objective is to find routes from the letters on the left of the 'river' to the matching letters on the right, e.g. **A** to **A**. Explain that the circles with words in them are like stepping stones.

2. Explain that students can only use a stepping stone if one of the two words contains the same vowel sound as the letter of the route they are following. For example, for the **A** *route*, the first stone contains the word face, which has the same vowel sound as the letter **A** - /eɪ/

3. As an example, work through the route for letter **A** as a whole class:
A - *face – rain – plate – wait – eight – days – plain – plane – gave* - **A**
Point out the interesting features of this route:

- There are several different ways of spelling this vowel sound: *a_e*; *ai*; *ay* and *eigh*.

- Sometimes, there are two words with different spelling but the same pronunciation, for example *plane* and *plain*.

4. Ask students to do the same for the remaining letters. Advise them to use different coloured pens or pencils to mark the routes for each letter if possible.

5. Check the answers together. Then ask students to identify the different spelling patterns for each alphabet vowel.

Answer Key

A *– face – rain – plate – wait – eight – days – plain – plane – gave –* **A**

E *– cheap – feet – piece – peace – feel – meet – heat – these –* **E**

I *– try – night – wine – guys – size – eyes – white –* **I**

O *– boat – cold – road – home – phone – coast – most – nose –* **O**

U *– true – tune – few – use – grew – two – boot – food – news –* **U**

Spellings:

A *– a_e, ai, ay, eigh*

E *– ea, ee, ie, e_e*

I *– y, igh, i_e, uy, eye*

O *– oa, o, o_e*

U *– ue, u_e, ew, wo, oo*

The letter **A**
Rhymes with say
Weigh and pay
And stay away

The letter **E**
Rhymes with see
Key and free
And three for tea

The letter **I**
Rhymes with fly
High and sky
And buy and bye

The letter **O**
Rhymes with know
Go and slow
And toe and so

The letter **U**
Rhymes with do
New and shoe
And blue and you

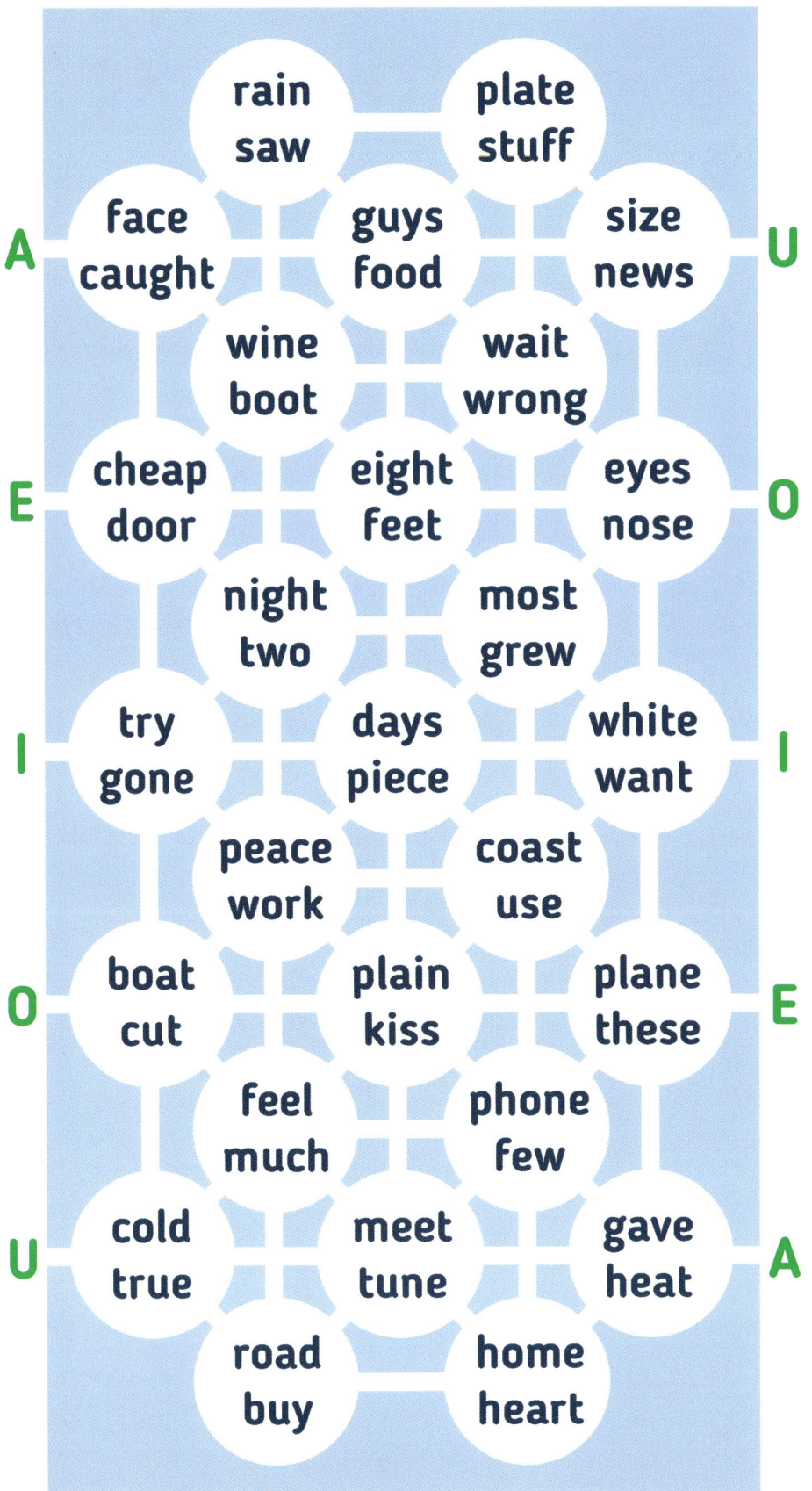

6.13

Money to Burn

TEACHING FOCUS

Pronouncing the vowel phoneme /ɜː/

MINIMUM LEVEL

Pre-Intermediate

ACTIVITY

Rap and Maze

WORKSHEETS

Print **Worksheet 6.13** for each student in the class.

AUDIO FILES

Audio 6.13-1

Background

The phoneme /ɜː/ is a long sound, made with jaw, tongue and lips all in a neutral position – all of the mouth muscles are slack. Sometimes people's mouths are in this position when they are trying to think, and so this is the sound that corresponds to the hesitation sounds often written as *ehm…* or *er….* It always comes before a letter *r* in a word, and this may or may not be pronounced. For example, in England the letter *r* in words like *girl* is not pronounced – in fact, we can consider the /ɜː/ to correspond to the spelling *ir*. In the USA, on the other hand, the tongue **does** curl back to form an /ɾ/ in words like *girl*. Students can choose whether or not to pronounce the /ɾ/, But either way, the letter *r* changes the vowel sound so that it becomes /ɜː/.

As regards spelling, there are a number of different ways of spelling /ɜː/, because the letter *r* neutralises the preceding vowel – so it may be spelt *ir, ur, er, or* or *ear* (*girl, nurse, serve, word, search*). The first two are the most common.

Language Comparison

For Brazilian learners, the vowel sound /ɜː/ is difficult because it doesn't exist in Portuguese. You will need to show them how the mouth muscles have to be relaxed and neutral. Equally problematic however is the fact that /ɜː/ can be spelt in so many different ways. Point out that the letter *r* in the spelling may or may not be pronounced, depending on the accent. They may choose to say it whichever way they prefer, but for listening, they will need to be ready for both!

Rap Activity

1. Give out **Worksheet 6.13**. Read out the poem and check understanding. Ask students what they think *money to burn* could mean (= *to have so much money that you waste it without worrying*).

   Alternatively, you can use **Audio 6.13-1**. Students might ask for the meaning of *rags* (= *clothes which are torn and dirty*).

2. Say each line and ask the class to repeat it. Listen and check their pronunciation, especially to the sound /ɜː/ (shown in green). Help students to pronounce this sound if necessary, and point out that it can be spelt in different ways.

3. Say each pair of lines and ask the class to repeat them.

4. Get the whole class in chorus to say the poem together, making sure the beat falls on the syllables in **bold**.

Maze Activity

1. Ask the students to look at the maze and find a route from **A** to **B**. Explain that they can go through a 'room' only if the word contains the sound /ɜː/.

2. Go through the first two or three words together as a class to get students started. Then leave them to work though it on their own.

3. Check the answers together.

4. Get students to say the words in the correct route, being careful to pronounce the same vowel sound in all. Then ask them to find all the different possible spellings of this sound: *ir, ur, er, or or ear.*

Answer Key

A – *burn, word, term, sir, search, third, work, heard, germ, nurse, world, first, church, bird, serve, birth, purse, fur, worst, early, girl, turn, certain, dirty, thirty* – **B**

The **girl** has a **lot** to **learn**
She **thinks** she's got **mon**ey to **burn**
She'll **emp**ty her **purse**
And **things**'ll get **worse**
And **mon**ey's not **eas**y to **earn**

One more **skirt** won't **hurt**
One more de**sign**er **shirt**
What**ev**er they're **worth**
They'll **cost** the **earth**
But **soon** they'll be **rags** in the **dirt**

A

burn	word	warm	birth	purse	fur
winter	term	sure	serve	there	worst
search	sir	church	bird	ear	early
third	fire	first	fair	turn	girl
work	warm	world	north	certain	near
heard	germ	nurse	news	dirty	thirty

B

Ambitions

6.14

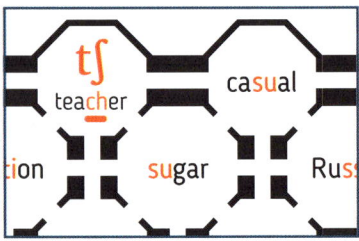

TEACHING FOCUS

Consonant spellings of /tʃ/, /ʃ/ and /ʒ/

MINIMUM LEVEL

Intermediate

ACTIVITY

Rap and Maze

WORKSHEETS

Print *Worksheet 6.14* for each student in the class.

AUDIO FILES

Audio 6.14-1

Audio 6.14-2

Background

The consonant /ʃ/ is similar to /s/ but with the tongue further back from the alveolar ridge. The typical spelling is *sh* (*fashion*).

The consonant /tʃ/ is a combination of /t/ followed by a /ʃ/ and the typical spelling is *ch* (*teacher*).

The consonant /ʒ/ is the same as /ʃ/ but voiced. It is not a common sound in English and the most common spelling is *S* (*vision*).

The focus of this lesson are the spelling patterns *T* or *S* (and *C*) followed by *U*, *I* or *E*, for example *future, station, sugar, passion, ocean*. These spelling patterns may correspond to the three consonant sounds described above.

Language Comparison

Brazilian learners often make mistakes in pronouncing the words with the spelling patterns described above. This is not because the phonemes are difficult to produce, but rather because the pronunciation is so difficult to guess from the spelling.

Rap Activity

1. Give out *Worksheet 6.14*. Read out the poem (it has the form of a rap) and check understanding. Alternatively, you can use *Audio 6.14-1* (or *Audio 14.2-2*, which is the backing music without the voice). Check students understand the word *ambition* (= *a strong desire to achieve something*).

2. Say each line and ask the class to repeat it. Listen and check their pronunciation, especially to the sounds /ʃ/, /tʃ/ and /ʒ/ (shown in red). Help them to pronounce these sounds if necessary, and point out the unusual spellings.

3. Say each pair of lines and ask the class to repeat them.

4. Get the whole class in chorus to say the poem together.

Maze Activity

1. Ask the students to look at the maze and find a routes from /ʃ/, /tʃ/ and /ʒ/ at the top to /ʃ/, /tʃ/ and /ʒ/ at the bottom. They can go through a 'room' only if the word contains the sound at the top of the route.

2. Go through the first two or three words together as a class to get students started. Then leave them to work though it on their own.

3. Check the answers together.

4. Get students to say the words in the correct route, being careful to pronounce the same consonant sound in all. Then ask them to find all the different possible spellings of this sound.

Answer Key

/ʃ/ – *fashion, patient, station, sugar, Russia, nation, ocean, delicious, action, sure, passion* – /ʃ/

/tʃ/ – *teacher, future, statue, picture, actual, culture, Christian, adventure, question* –/tʃ/

/ʒ/ – *vision, casual, measure, usual, leisure, decision, pleasure, illusion, treasure* – /ʒ/

What's your pleasure
Work or leisure?
Do you have a passion
For literature or fashion?

Make a big decision
Or watch the television?
Summer education
Or just a long vacation?

Have a great ambition
To join an expedition?
Or do you feel ambitious
To cook something delicious?

Do you have a notion
To sail across an ocean?
Or study art and culture
And learn to paint a picture?

Wanted, Needed

6.15

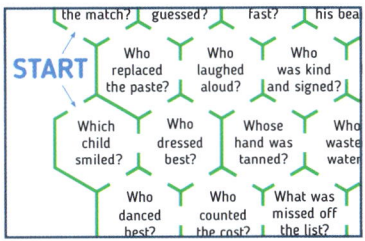

Background

The pronunciation of the past tense suffix –ed varies depending on the phoneme it comes after. If the root verb ends with /t/ or /d/ (for example *want*, *need*), the –ed is /ɪd/. Notice that this includes a vowel phoneme, which means that the suffix is an extra syllable. *Wait* and *need* are one syllable but *waited* and *needed* are two. If the root verb ends with any voiceless consonant except /t/ (for example, *hope*, *look*, *laugh*, *miss*, *wash*, *watch*), then the –ed is /t/ – not an extra syllable. *Hope* is one syllable, *hoped* is also one syllable. If the root verb ends with any other consonant or vowel phoneme, the –ed is /d/, and again, it is not an extra syllable: *close* is one syllable, *closed* is one syllable.

The most important rule is the first, when the –ed is /ɪd/, because adding an extra syllable makes a big difference. The difference between the /t/ or /d/ endings is not so big and students will usually be intelligible with either.

Note: Although I've called this –ed the past tense suffix, it is also common in past participles as well as adjectives such as *annoyed*, and the same pronunciation rules apply.

Language Comparison

A big problem which Portuguese-speaking students often have relates to spelling. They often pronounce the past tense suffix as the extra syllable /ɪd/ for all the verbs, because they see the vowel *e* in the spelling and expect that it should be pronounced. Point out that pairs of words like *child* and *smiled* rhyme, despite the fact that one of them has an *e* and the other doesn't.

Rap Activity

1. Give out **Worksheet 6.15**. Read out the poem (it has the form of a rap) and check understanding. Alternatively, you can use **Audio 6.15–1** (or **Audio 6.15–2**, which is the backing music without the voice).

2. Say each line and ask the class to repeat it. Listen and check student's pronunciation, especially of the –ed endings.

3. Ask students to read the rule given in the last two lines of the poem. Then ask them to look again at the rest of the poem and underline the words where the *e* is pronounced in the *–ed* ending.
(**Answer:** *wanted, needed, succeeded, ended, mended, waited, hated, lifted, started*).

4. Say each pair of lines and ask the class to repeat them.

6. Get the whole class in chorus to say the poem together.

Maze Activity

1. Ask the students to look at the maze and find a route from *Start* to *End*. They can go through a 'room' only if the sentence contains two words which rhyme, for example *showed* and *road*. Point out that rhyme means that the ends of the two words (the vowel and consonant) are pronounced the same – *even if the spelling is different*!

2. Go through the first one or two 'rooms' together as a class to get them started. Then leave them to work though it on their own. Point out that they can only pass though a door, not through a wall. So for example, they can't go directly from *Start* to *Who replaced the paste?*

3. Check the answers together.

4. Get students to read out the sentences in the correct route, being careful to pronounce the rhymes correctly.

Answer Key

START – *Which child smiled?, Who dressed best?, Who replaced the paste?, Which guest guessed?, What passed fast?, Who played and paid?, Who crossed and lost?, Who feared his beard?, Who was kind and signed?, Whose hand was tanned?, What was missed off the list?, Who planned to stand?, Who was sacked in fact?* – **END**

Wanted, needed
Tried, succeeded

Closed and locked
Pleased or shocked

Finished, ended
Fixed or mended

Lifted, dropped
Started, stopped

Walked or waited
Loved or hated

In the past, pronounce the E
Only after D or T!

Rhyme Maze

Only enter if two of the words rhyme!

Who sh**owe**d us the r**oad**? → **rhyme**

START

END

Who phoned the most?

What passed fast?

Who played and paid?

Who crossed and lost?

Who watched the match?

Which guest guessed?

Who acted fast?

Who feared his beard?

Who loved and lost?

Who replaced the paste?

Who laughed aloud?

Who was kind and signed?

Who faced the facts?

Which child smiled?

Who dressed best?

Whose hand was tanned?

Who wasted water?

Who was sacked in fact?

Who danced best?

Who counted the cost?

What was missed off the list?

Who planned to stand?

Stress Wall

6.16

restaurant and asks for the menu.
n't serve animals'
serve people?'
the waiter.
ile,
nose then!'

TEACHING FOCUS

Word stress in cognates; syllable reduction

MINIMUM LEVEL

Pre-Intermediate

ACTIVITY

Joke and Maze

WORKSHEETS

Print **Worksheet 6.16** for each student in the class.

AUDIO FILES

Audio 6.16–1 ⏸ ↺

Audio 6.16–2 ⏸ ↺

Background

In words of more than one syllable, one of the syllables is stressed. It is very often the first, for example *crocodile*, but not always – for example *banana*. In the syllables which are <u>not</u> stressed, the vowel sound is often reduced to the sound /ə/ (known as the *schwa*). For example, *crocodile* is /ˈkrɒkədaɪl/, and *banana* is /bəˈnɑːnə/. This vowel reduction helps to emphasise the stressed syllable, and reduces the amount of muscular effort required to say the word. In some words, the vowel may be reduced so much that it can disappear altogether. For example, the letters *au* in the word restaurant may be pronounced as a schwa, or not at all, making it a two-syllable word /ˈrestrɒnt/.

Vowel reduction is very common in native varieties of English, and students need to be aware of it for listening. However, it isn't usually essential for intelligibility.

Language Comparison

Portuguese words often have the word stress later in the word than in English. It isn't so common to place the stress on the first syllable. The difference is very noticeable in words which are very similar in the two languages, such as *crocodile* and *crocodilo* – the English has the stress on the first syllable while the Portuguese has the stress on the third.

One difficulty for Brazilian learners of English is that they have to remember not to apply the same stress patterns to cognate words such as this in English. Most of the words in Lesson 16 are cognates like this.

A second difficulty relates to vowel spelling. Portuguese speaking learners may fully pronounce the vowel letters in words instead of using a schwa. For example, they may try to fully pronounce both of the letters *OU* in *curious*, while in English, these are reduced to a simple /ə/.

Joke Activity

1. Give out **Worksheet 6.16**. Explain that the text at the top of the page is a joke. Tell students to read it and find the misunderstanding. You could give a clue: the phrase We don't serve animals has two possible meanings (**Answer:** *The waiter means that they don't serve customers who are animals; the crocodile 'understands' that animals are not on the menu*).

2. Ask students to read the text again and underline words which are the same, or nearly the same, in Portuguese (**Answer:** *crocodile, restaurant, animals, excellent*).

3. Read out the text or play *Audio 6.16-1*. (If you read out the text yourself, note that *restaurant* may be pronounced with two or three syllables). Ask students to listen especially to the words they underlined and answer this question: *How is the English pronunciation different from the Portuguese?* Elicit that the stress pattern is different. All of the words have the stress on the first syllable in English. In Portuguese, the stress is near the end.

4. Read out the four words *crocodile, restaurant, animals* and, *excellent*. Ask students to say how many syllables there are in each. Point out that *restaurant* may be pronounced with two or three syllables – the second vowel sound may be cut. Encourage students to try saying the words with the vowel sound cut, to make them more aware of this.

5. Ask students in pairs or groups to practice saying the joke aloud, paying attention to the pronunciation of the underlined words. Then ask them to tell a second version of the joke, replacing *crocodile* with *elephant* and *people* with *vegetables*.

Maze Activity

1. Tell the students to look at the maze and find a route from Start to End. They can go through a 'room' only if the word has the stress on the first syllable. They can go through 'doors' (gaps in the line), not through walls.

2. Go through the first two or three words together as a class to get them started. Then leave students to work though it on their own. **Note:** although many of the words look higher than A2 level, they are almost all the same or similar to Portuguese words, so they should look familiar.

3. Check the answers together. Check that students pronounce the stress on the first syllable.

4. The underlined words in the answer key may all have the second vowel sound cut. Read out the words (or play *Audio 6.16-2*) and ask students to say which ones have a vowel sound cut (underlined in the key below).

5. Students practice pronouncing the words themselves.

Answer Key

Start – *restaurant*, *crocodile, animal, African, excellent, chocolate, photograph, million, cereal, bicycle, hospital, generous, different, natural, delicate, telephone, curious, possible, innocent, company, positive, separate, organize, festival, family* – **End**

A crocodile crawls into a restaurant and asks for the menu.

The waiter says, 'Sorry we don't serve animals'

The crocodile says 'Do you serve people?'

'Of course!', says the waiter.

'Excellent' says the crocodile,

'I'll have one of those then!'

Which words have stress on the first syllable?

START	information	animal	African	excellent
restaurant	crocodile	American	chocolate	
society	banana	bicycle	adventure	photograph
generous	hospital	cereal	million	
different	disaster	democracy	separate	intelligent
natural	university	positive	organise	
delicate	creative	company	familiar	festival
telephone	innocent	television	family	
curious	possible	important	original	END

Tennis Shoes

6.17

tennis shoes
compound noun

TEACHING FOCUS

Word stress in compound nouns

MINIMUM LEVEL

Intermediate

ACTIVITY

Choral chant/drill

WORKSHEETS

Print **Worksheet 6.17** for each student in the class

AUDIO FILES

Audio 6.17–1

Audio 6.17–2

Background

In English, the stress tends to fall on the first syllable in nouns. The same is true when the noun is made up of two joined parts, such as *surfboard*, or two parts which are not joined such as *tennis shoes*.

Notice that *tennis shoes* behaves like a single word, with the stress on the first part, while *red shoes* is two different words, an adjective and a noun, both stressed. The difference is clear in this example, but sometimes the difference is less clear. For example *car keys* is a compound with stress on *car* and *car door* is two words, both stressed. However, the examples in this lesson are only compounds like *car keys*, so there is no need to go into this difficulty.

Language Comparison

In Portuguese, the stress tends to go on the last part of the phrase. Compare *surfboard* (with the stress on *surf*) and *prancha de surfe* (with the stress on *surfe*). Students often transfer this to English, incorrectly stressing the last part of the compound. They are more likely to make this mistake when the stressed syllable is a long way from the end of the phrase, for example *parachute jumping* (the stress is 5 syllables from the end) or *horse-riding instructor* (the stress is 6 syllables from the end).

Introductory Activity

1. Give out **Worksheet 6.17** . Ask students to look at the photograph and explain the misunderstanding (**Answer:** the woman on the left has shortened the phrase *tennis shoes* to *tennis*, as in Brazilian Portuguese. The woman on the right thinks she's asking about the sport, not the shoes).

2. Point out the pictures of the two pairs of shoes and compare the pronunciation. When you say red shoes, stress both words. When you say tennis shoes, stress only the first syllable, as if the whole phrase is a single word. Get students to practice pronouncing the two phrases.

Workout Activity

1. Demonstrate chanting *shoes, gym shoes, tennis shoes*, keeping time with three hand claps. Alternatively, use *Audio 6.17–1*.

You could also draw this diagram on the board to show how the number of syllables increases:

shoes	gym shoes	tennis shoes
O	Oo	Ooo

2. Repeat the chant **shoes**, **gym** shoes, **ten**nis shoes, keeping time with three hand claps, and ask the students to repeat after you, keeping the same rhythm.

3. Now do the same thing for **1 – 6** of the entire **EASY** *section*. Notice that the word groups get a little more difficult towards the end, because there are more syllables to say. If students are finding it too difficult, go slower.

For more challenge, go faster. *Audio 6.17–2* contains a demonstration of all three sections of the workout.

4. **Optional activity 1**: Divide the class into three groups **A**, **B** and **C**. Keeping the clapping rhythm, each group chants one of the words, for example:

Group A: *shoes!*

Group B: *gym shoes!*

Group C: *tennis shoes!*

5. **Optional activity 2**: (Memory game) Ask the students to work in pairs or small groups. One student looks at the page and the other(s) cover it. The first student says the first two words of the word groups and the other(s) have to say the third from memory. They should always stress the first syllable. For example:

Student A: *shoes, gym shoes…*

Student(s) B: *tennis shoes!*

6. Repeat *Step 3* and any of the optional *Steps 4* and *5* for the remaining sections; **HARD 1 – 6** and **EXTRA 1 – 6**.

6.17 Tennis Shoes

Do you like my tennis?

I haven't seen you play yet!

red **shoes**
adjective   noun

tennis shoes
compound noun

easy

1
shoes
gym shoes
tennis shoes

2
skates
ice-skates
roller skates

3
boots
walking boots
basketball boots

4
ball
football
basketball

5
bat
cricket bat
baseball bat

6
racket
tennis racket
badminton racket

hard

1
cap
flat cap
baseball cap

2
goggles
ski goggles
swimming goggles

3
helmet
bike helmet
motorbike helmet

4
bike
road bike
mountain bike

5
board
skateboard
windsurfing board

6
contest
surfing contest
windsurfing contest

extra

1
diving
sky diving
scuba diving

2
climbing
rock climbing
mountain climbing

3
jumping
bungee jumping
parachute jumping

4
coach
football coach
basketball coach

5
driver
racing driver
ambulance driver

6
in**struc**tor
fitness instructor
horse-riding instructor

I Love You

TEACHING FOCUS
Tonic Stress

MINIMUM LEVEL
Pre-Intermediate

ACTIVITY
Choral chant/drill

WORKSHEETS
Print one copy of **Worksheet 6.18** for each student in the class.

AUDIO FILES

Audio 6.18-1

Audio 6.18-2

Background

In English, sentences (or more accurately, phrases) are spoken with one syllable given extra emphasis. This is known as tonic stress, and it serves to make the word containing that syllable more noticeable. A speaker may choose to put the tonic stress anywhere in the phrase, depending on meaning. However, the most common position is on the last content word of the phrase. (Words like verbs, nouns and adjectives are *content* words. These contrast with *grammar* words such as pronouns and prepositions). So, for example, in *I love you* the most likely word to be stressed is *love*. The speaker would only stress the final pronoun *you* in order to create a contrast, with some other person for example.

Language Comparison

In Portuguese, speakers are more likely to place the tonic stress on the last word in the phrase. Students often transfer this to English, placing the stress on the last word even when it is a grammar word. For example, they may say *I love you* with the stress on *you*. This can create an unintended meaning, leading to misunderstanding.

Students are more likely to make this mistake when the stressed syllable is a long way from the end of the phrase. For example, in *I love you*, the normal stress is only one syllable away from the end, but in *I owe it to you*, it is four syllables from the end – they are likely to find the second sentence more difficult than the first.

Introductory Activity

1. Give out **Worksheet 6.18**. Ask students to look at the photograph and explain the misunderstanding (**Answer:** the person on the left is saying *I love you*, she means the pronoun *'you'*, not the person on the right!).

2. Ask students how they could use punctuation to make the meaning of 'I love you' clearer in the picture (**Answer:** Put quotation marks around the word *'you'*).

3. Explain about stress in sentences and check students understand. Get them to try saying the phrase *I love you* first with the normal stress on *love*, and then with the special stress on *you*.

Workout Activity

1. This workout has the form of a chant. Each of the lines **1 – 8** has four beats, but there are increasing numbers of unstressed syllables between each beat as you go from left to right. Play *Audio 6.18-1* or say the chant yourself (fill in the correct answers on your copy of the worksheet first). Tell students to fill in the missing words in each line.

Answers: 1 *feel*, **2** *send*, **3** *looked*, **4** *see*, **5** *tell*, **6** *pay*, **7** *help*, **8** *ask*.

2. Say each line and ask the class to repeat it. Listen and check their pronunciation, especially to the correct stress placement in each sentence shown in **bold**. Notice that the words in *red* are the unstressed syllables which come after the main stress in each sentence. These are represented in the *red circles* at the top of each column.

3. Get the whole class in chorus to say the chant together, making sure the beat falls on the syllables in **bold**. They could clap the rhythm, with four claps for each line.

4. Say sentences from the chant either with the 'normal' stress (on the word in **bold**) or with 'special' stress (<u>not on</u> the word in **bold**). Ask students to say if your sentence is 'normal' or 'special'.

For example:

> **You:** *I* **owe** *it to you.*
>
> **Students:** *Normal!*
>
> **You:** *You'll write to* **me***.*
>
> **Students:** *Special!*

Alternatively, use *Audio 6.18-2* for this activity. These are the sentences on the audio:

> I **owe** it to you   *(normal)*;
> You'll write to **me**   *(special)*;
> I **can** wave to them   *(special)*;
> I can **give** it to them   *(normal)*;
> Will you **tell** it to her?   *(normal)*;
> Will **you** pay for them?   *(special)*;
> Can I work with **you**?   *(special)*;
> Did they **get** it from us?   *(normal)*

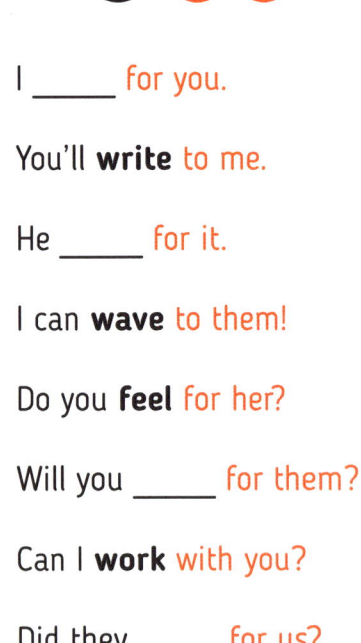

1	I **love** you!	I _____ for you.	I **owe** it to you!	I **do**!
2	You'll **text** me.	You'll **write** to me.	You'll _____ it to me.	You **will**!
3	He **liked** it.	He _____ for it.	He **found** it for me.	He **did**!
4	I can _____ them!	I can **wave** to them!	I can **give** it to them!	I **can**!
5	Do you **love** her?	Do you **feel** for her?	Will you _____ it to her?	I **will**!
6	Will you **get** them?	Will you _____ for them?	Will you **keep** them for me?	I **will**!
7	Can I _____ you?	Can I **work** with you?	Can I **bring** it for you?	I **can**!
8	Did they **want** us?	Did they _____ for us?	Did they **get** it from us?	They **did**!

PronPack Sound Charts

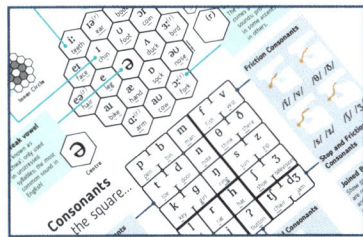

Vowel Charts 1 & 2

The **Vowel Charts** on this page provide a quick and easy comparison between the IPA symbols often used in UK publications and the vowel symbols found in many US publications.

PronPack Infographic

The **PronPack Sound Chart Infographic** on the next page explains how the Sound Chart is organised and provides a key to the phonemic symbols used in this book.

Note: Printable versions of all the **PronPack Sound Charts** can be found at www.pronpack.com

1. IPA Vowel Symbols (often used in UK publications)

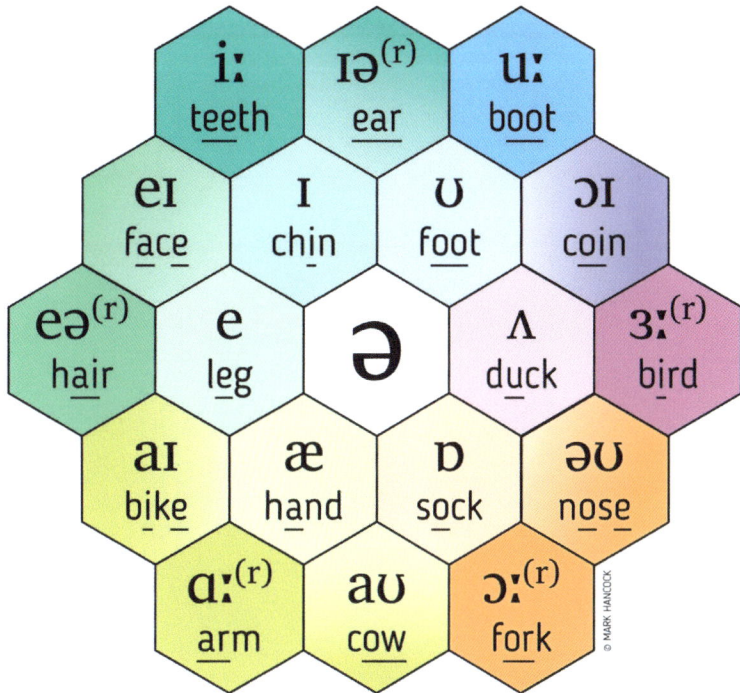

2. Alternative Vowel Symbols (often used in US publications)

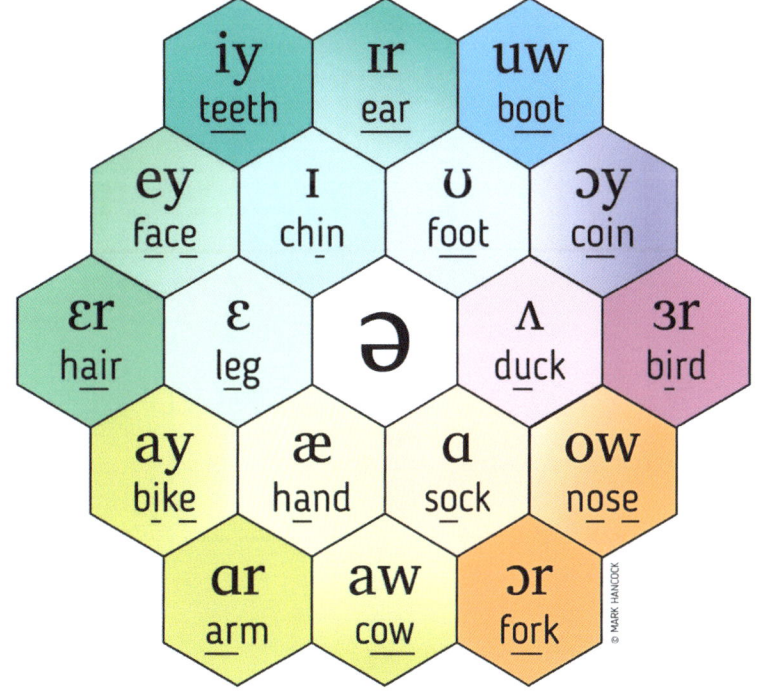

Pronunciation of English for
Brazilian learners

Vowels
in the hexagon...

Six Long vowels
Symbols usually have : but /eə/ also considered a long vowel in this model.

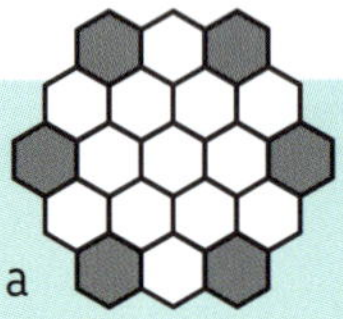

Outer Circle

Corners

Six Short vowels
Symbols are all single; these vowels never end a syllable.

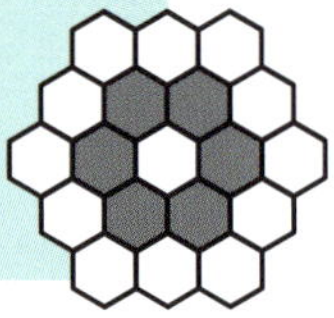

Inner Circle

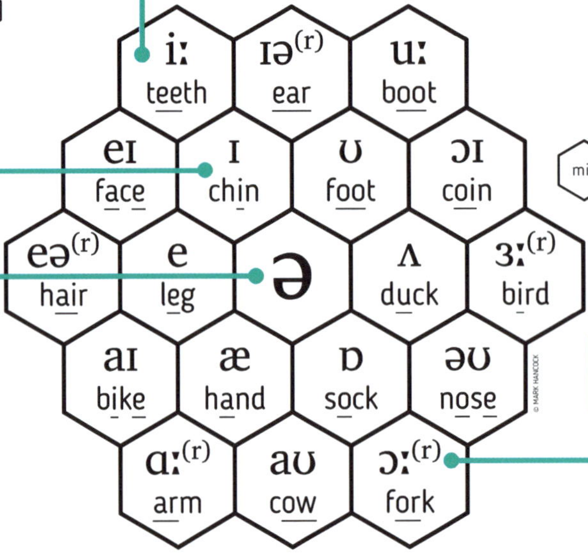

Six Diphthongs
Symbols have two elements; the sound moves from one position to the other.

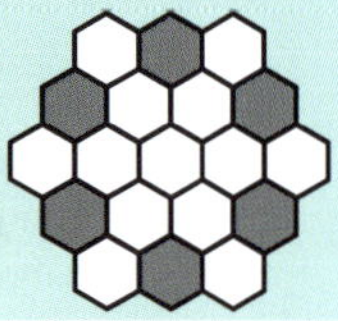

Sides

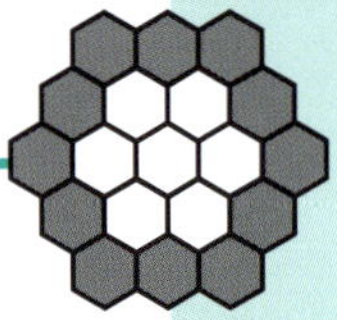

The weak vowel
Also known as 'schwa'; only used in unstressed syllables; the most common sound in English!

Hexagon chart (vowels):

- iː — teeth
- ɪə⁽ʳ⁾ — ear
- uː — boot
- eɪ — face
- ɪ — chin
- ʊ — foot
- ɔɪ — coin
- eə⁽ʳ⁾ — hair
- e — leg
- ə
- ʌ — duck
- ɜː⁽ʳ⁾ — bird
- aɪ — bike
- æ — hand
- ɒ — sock
- əʊ — nose
- ɑː⁽ʳ⁾ — arm
- aʊ — cow
- ɔː⁽ʳ⁾ — fork

© MARK HANCOCK

ə

Centre

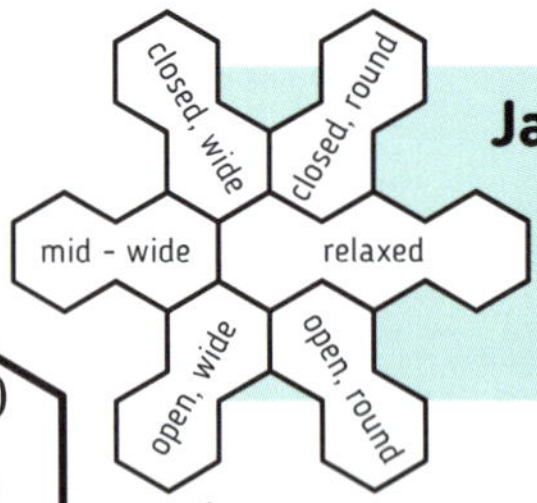

Jaw and lip positions
- closed, wide
- closed, round
- mid – wide
- relaxed
- open, wide
- open, round

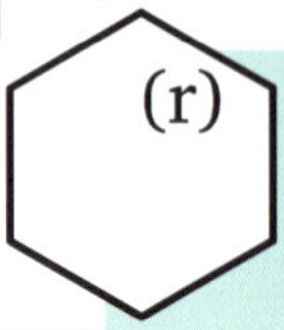

Optional r
(r) The letter **r** usually comes after these sounds; pronounced in some accents, not in others.

Consonants
in the square...

p — pen	b — bin	m — man	f — fish	v — vest
t — toe	d — door	n — note	θ — think	ð — there
k — key	g — girl	ŋ — ring	s — sun	z — zip
l — leaf	r — rat	h — hat	ʃ — shoe	ʒ — television
w — watch	j — year	ʔ — button	tʃ — chair	dʒ — jam

Stop Consonants
/p/
/b/
/m/

/t/
/d/
/n/

/k/
/g/
/ŋ/

Friction Consonants
/f/ /v/   /θ/ /ð/

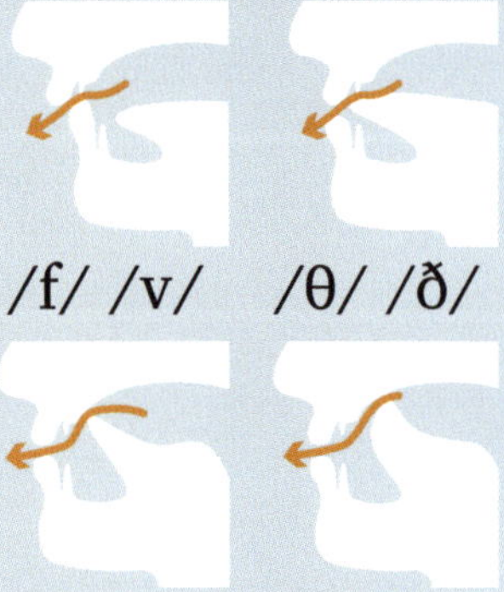

/s/ /z/   /ʃ/ /ʒ/

Stop and Friction Consonants

Vowel-like Consonants
Have little or no obstruction.

Glottal Consonants

Joined Boxes
Show pairs of sounds which are related but one is voiced and the other isn't.

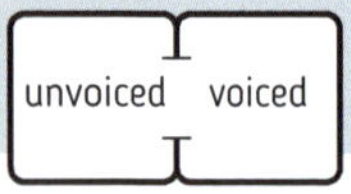

unvoiced | voiced

About the Author

Mark Hancock is a well-known ELT author and teacher with over 30 years experience in Sudan, Turkey, Brazil, and in Spain. Pronunciation has been a special interest for much of his career, and he has written several popular, award-winning textbooks on the topic. Many teachers find pronunciation to be a daunting aspect of language teaching, and Mark's approach has always been to engage and inspire the learner, creating materials and tasks which are practical and enjoyable for both teachers and students.

Mark regularly presents about pronunciation at conferences, and trains teachers through workshops and short courses, both face-to-face and online. In his free time, he is a keen artist and musician and also enjoys walking in the mountains.

By the same author

- *Mark Hancock's 50 Tips for Teaching Pronunciation* (CUP 2020)
- *PronPack 1-5* (Hancock McDonald ELT 2017)
- *Authentic Listening Resource Pack* (Delta 2014, co-authored with Annie McDonald)
- *English Pronunciation in Use Intermediate* (CUP 2003, 2012)
- *English Result 1-4* (OUP 2007-2010 co-authored with Annie McDonald)
- *Pen Pictures 1-3* (OUP 1999-2000 co-authored with Annie McDonald)
- *Singing Grammar* (CUP 1999)
- *Pronunciation Games* (CUP 1995)

Acknowledgements

My first book, *Pronunciation Games*, was published back in 1995 by *Cambridge University Press* and designed by my sister. It seems appropriate that all these years later, my self-published *PronPack* collection should also be pronunciation activities, again produced in collaboration with Amanda.

A huge thank you is also due to Annie McDonald for her editorial work and tireless encouragement. Thanks also to Ricardo Sili for his help, advice and feedback and to Henry Wong of Heliographic for his graphic design input.

Lastly I'd like to thank Taylor Veigga for helping to trial the material in this book and providing feedback.

The PronPack Collection

Other titles published by Hancock McDonald ELT

PronPack is a growing collection of innovative teacher's resource materials for working on English pronunciation in the classroom. **PronPacks 1-4** won the 2018 *ELTons Award for Innovation in Teacher Resources*, as well as the *English Speaking Union's 2018 English Language Award runner-up for teacher resources.*

PronPack 1: Pronunciation Workouts
Print ISBN: 9780995757516
eBook ISBN: 9780995757554

PronPack 2: Pronunciation Puzzles
Print ISBN: 9780995757523
eBook ISBN: 9780995757561

PronPack 3: Pronunciation Pairworks
Print ISBN: 9780995757530
eBook ISBN: 9780995757578

PronPack 4: Pronunciation Poems
Print ISBN: 9780995757547
eBook ISBN: 9780995757585

PronPack 5: Pronunciation of English for Spanish speakers
Print ISBN: 9780995757509
eBook ISBN: 9780995757592

PronPack 6: Pronunciation of English for Brazilian learners
Print ISBN: 9781838404000
eBook ISBN: 9781838404017

Hancock McDonald
ENGLISH LANGUAGE TEACHING

Printed in Great Britain
by Amazon